NOIR CITY
OFFICIAL MAGAZINE OF THE FILM NOIR FOUNDATION

ANNUAL SIXTEEN

The Best of **NOIR CITY** Magazine

2023

PUBLISHED BY THE FILM NOIR FOUNDATION
San Francisco | Los Angeles | New York

NOIR CITY ANNUAL 16: The Best of NOIR CITY 2023

Copyright © 2024 by the Film Noir Foundation. All rights reserved. Printed in the United States of America. No part of this book may be used or reproduced in any manner whatsoever without written permission except in the case of brief quotations embedded in critical articles or reviews. For additional information, contact the Film Noir Foundation, 1411 Paru Street, Alameda, CA 94501 or visit filmnoirfoundation.org.

All proceeds from the sale of this book go directly to the non-profit Film Noir Foundation's mission to find and preserve *films noir* in danger of deterioration, damage or loss, and to ensure that high quality prints of these classic films remain in circulation for, we hope, theatrical exhibition to future generations.

Interested in contributing to *NOIR CITY Magazine*? Contact us at mailbox@filmnoirfoundation.org. Accepted submissions are published with the permission of the authors and the Film Noir Foundation claims no exclusive rights to the material.

FIRST EDITION

Cover and book design by Michael Kronenberg

ISBN 978-0-9822973-2-2

FRONT COVER: *This Gun for Hire* (1942), one-sheet poster
FRONTISPIECE: Bette Davis in *The Letter* (1940)
BACK COVER: *Dark Passage* (1947), Italian poster

INTRODUCTION

AMERICA'S TRUE GDP: CRIME

In the 1952 crime thriller *The Turning Point*, Edmond O'Brien plays a special prosecutor determined to bring down a regional crime boss (Ed Begley) who has hidden his larceny behind an array of legitimate fronts. During a televised hearing in which O'Brien's committee questions the glib and arrogant crook, the prosecutor declares that corruption must be rooted out at the local level to prevent it from infecting society like a cancer. "How far will it go?" O'Brien asks rhetorically, "All the way to the White House?"

It took a while, but that question has been definitely answered. One candidate in the 2024 U.S. presidential election, Donald Trump, alleged in the first debate of the campaign that incumbent President Joseph Biden was a criminal who belonged behind bars. For some reason, Biden chose not to point out that his opponent was the only convicted felon onstage that night and that his Republican rival's quest for a second term in the White House represented his best bet for evading a prison sentence. Whatever the election's results, it is inarguable that a large portion of the U.S. citizenry will believe, either through facts or fabrication, that the nation's Commander-in-Chief is a criminal.

Many Americans are perplexed at how the world's leading beacon of democracy has gotten itself into a position where the only options for leadership are a doddering lifetime legislator, perceived by his rivals as an American Dr. Mabuse, or a legendarily corrupt "businessman" who has failed at every commercial venture except being a reality-TV star and the President of the United States—roles that are now hopelessly entwined in public consciousness.

Are we really surprised it's come to this? After all, America's gross domestic product is, and always has been, Crime.

If you don't believe me, just peruse a daily paper—if you can still find one. Newspapers have long been divided into five sections: "News" could now be more precisely called "Crime and Corruption," since that's what lurks behind every national story involving politics and economics. The "Metro" section features local news—typically a litany of murder and manslaughter and the occasional tragic accident. "Sports"—once a respite—can barely camouflage the rampant greed of billionaire owners and violent abuses of star athletes. The "Business" section—where the most egregious crimes are on display—is beyond the comprehension of John Q. Public (which is why white-collar perps run rampant). The ever-shrinking "Arts & Entertainment" section once offered sanctuary. But these days, most of the stories we're being told—if they aren't superhero fantasies—are "Based on a True Story." And 99% of those stories involve crime, be it institutional or intimate.

I've long maintained that the original noir era, an explosion of artist-inspired creativity in the wake of the Great Depression and World War II, represented the on-screen expression of America's loss of innocence. In the first paragraph of the first book I ever wrote on the subject, I called many of these films "warning flares launched by artists working the night shift at the Dream Factory." The irony is that they were made during a time when the Production Code policed what was considered appropriate viewing. Movies based on true crimes were few and far between—not because there weren't heinous crimes committed daily in this country, but because in the studio era there was a much closer connection between the federal government, Wall Street, and Hollywood. Control was exerted over the stories presented to the public, and those stories reflected who we *wanted* to be, more than who we actually were.

Back then, artists didn't advertise that a story was based on fact. The notorious 1928 case of adulterous murderer Ruth Snyder may have inspired James M. Cain to write *The Postman Always Rings Twice* (published in 1934, not made into a Hollywood film until 1946), but neither its publisher, Alfred Knopf, nor Metro-Goldwyn-Mayer promoted the book or film as "Based on a true story." The same held true for many classic works of noir, literary and cinematic. Writers would be intrigued by an actual crime and adapt it into a fictionized narrative. Sensitive readers and viewers could always assure themselves these tales were merely dark fantasies. They didn't have anything to do with our family, friends, and colleagues. Right?

Things began to change during the noir era, and that's what we explored in several in-depth NOIR CITY articles in 2023. I offered a survey of "true crime" movies from the classic era. Editor Imogen Sara Smith brought her typically keen insight to a consideration of how the visual representation of crime evolved over the years. Danilo Castro (clearly the star of this annual collection) looked at an array of cold cases that have gotten big-screen treatments. Did you know *Targets* (1968), *10 Rillington Place* (1971), and *Dog Day Afternoon* (1975) are all based on true crimes? We provide the factual backstories on these landmark movies.

I wish we could say that America heeded those mid-twentieth-century "warning flares." The fact that there's no escape from crime, in our lives or in our entertainment, would seem to indicate that Americans aren't good learners. Or maybe we're just criminals at heart.

—*Eddie Muller*

THE CRITERION CHANNEL

criterionchannel.com

The Lady from Shanghai (1947), directed by Orson Welles

NOIR CITY

PUBLISHER
Eddie Muller

EDITOR-IN-CHIEF
Imogen Sara Smith

MANAGING EDITORS
Danilo Castro
Steve Kronenberg

ART DIRECTOR/DESIGNER
Michael Kronenberg

**PROMOTIONAL DIRECTOR
EDITING/PRINT PRODUCTION**
Daryl Sparks

COPY EDITOR
Rachel Walther

NEWS EDITOR
Anne M. Hockens

EDITOR-AT-LARGE
Alan K. Rode

WEB MASTER
Ted Whipple

**FILM NOIR FOUNDATION
BOARD OF DIRECTORS**
Foster Hirsch
Brian Hollins
Andrea Kasin
Anita Monga
Eddie Muller, President
Alan K. Rode

ADVISORY COUNCIL
Gwen Deglise
Dana Delany
James Ellroy
Bruce Goldstein
Vince Keenan
John Kirk
Dennis Lehane
Leonard Maltin
Rose McGowan
Jon Mysel
Greg Olson
Fernando Martín Peña
Michael Schlesinger
Imogen Sara Smith
Todd Wiener

You've seen the movie... now read the book!

MURRAY FORBES
Hollow Triumph
Directed by Steve Sekely, starring Paul Henreid & Joan Bennett (1948)

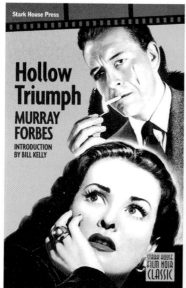

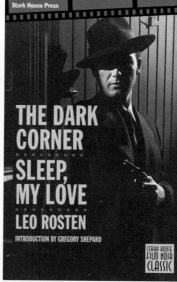

LEO ROSTEN
The Dark Corner
Directed by Henry Hathaway, starring Mark Stevens, Lucille Ball & Clifton Webb (1946)

Sleep, My Love
Directed by Douglas Sirk, starring Claudette Colbert, Robert Cummings & Don Ameche (1948)

JAMES GUNN
Born to Kill
Directed by Robert Wise, starring Lawrence Tierney & Claire Trevor (1947)

GERALD BUTLER
Kiss the Blood Off My Hands
Directed by Norman Foster, starring Joan Fontaine & Burt Lancaster (1948)

STARK HOUSE PRESS
1315 H Street, Eureka, CA 95501
707-498-3135 www.StarkHousePress.com

Available from your local bookstore or direct from the publisher.

"We are going to kill one passenger a minute until New York City pays 1 million dollars."

"THE TAKING OF PELHAM ONE TWO THREE"

Everyone read it.
Now you can live it.

PALOMAR PICTURES and PALLADIUM PRODUCTIONS presents
"THE TAKING OF PELHAM ONE TWO THREE"
starring
WALTER MATTHAU
ROBERT SHAW
MARTIN BALSAM
HECTOR ELIZONDO
Produced by
GABRIEL KATZKA and EDGAR J. SCHERICK
Screenplay by PETER STONE
Based on the novel by JOHN GODEY • Music DAVID SHIRE
Directed by JOSEPH SARGENT

TABLE OF CONTENTS

ESSAYS

26 **Stoner Noir**
By Danilo Castro

38 **No Exit**
How Franz Kafka's Dark Fable Became
Orson Welles's Masterwork
By Rachel Walther

46 **Architects of Illusion**
The Art Directors
By Jake Hinkson

60 **The Naked Eye**
Realism and the True Crime Aesthetic
By Imogen Sara Smith

70 **Bury the Past**
Land Swindles. Chicago Mobsters. A Prison Break. And America's Cosmetics Kingpin? Take a wild ride through the tumultuous story of Roger Touhy, Gangster.
By John Wranovics

78 **Ripped From the Headlines!**
By Eddie Muller

90 **Born to Lose**
Dog Day Afternoon's Many Realities
By Rachel Walther

100 **Burden of Proof**
Cold Case Noir
By Danilo Castro

118 **Guns for Hire**
A Chronological Survey of the Hit Man in Film Noir
By Danilo Castro

130 **Cruel Yule**
Noir and the Holiday Season
By Jeremy Arnold

TABLE OF CONTENTS

PROFILES

142 **Unhinged**
Timothy Carey's Wild Ride Through Noir and Beyond
By Steve Kronenberg

150 **Walter Matthau**
Noir's Rumpled Icon
By Vince Keenan

162 **Jean Hagen's Trail of Broken Dreams**
By Steve Kronenberg

170 **Noir by Any Name**
The Crime Dramas of Bob Rafelson
By Peter Tonguette

APPRECIATIONS

182 **Blood Over the Atlantic**
Nick Gomez's Eastern Seaboard Trilogy
By Rachel Walther

190 **Prime Cuts: My Favorite Neo-Noir**
Rolling Thunder
By Wallace Stroby

196 **Prime Cuts: My Favorite Neo-Noir**
10 Rillington Place
By Andy Wolverton

200 **Prime Cuts: My Favorite Neo-Noir**
Deep Cover
By Adam Nayman

204 **Noir or Not:** *Straw Dogs*
By Thomas Burchfield

208 **Noir or Not:** *Targets*
By Steve Kronenberg

214 **Book vs. Film:** *Sweet Smell of Success*
By Ben Terrall

THE BESTSELLING AUTHOR OF *NOIR BAR*
AND HOST OF TCM'S "NOIR ALLEY"

DARK CITY

THE LOST WORLD OF FILM NOIR
(REVISED AND EXPANDED EDITION)

Named by *The Hollywood Reporter* one of the
"100 Greatest Film Books of All Time!"

This revised and expanded edition of Eddie Muller's *Dark City* is a film noir lover's bible, taking readers on a tour of the urban landscape of the grim and gritty genre in a definitive, highly illustrated volume.

AVAILABLE NOW WHEREVER BOOKS ARE SOLD!

ALSO AVAILABLE

**KID NOIR: KITTY FERAL
AND THE CASE OF THE
MARSHMALLOW MONKEY
BY EDDIE MULLER
& JESSICA SCHMIDT**

TCM
TURNER CLASSIC MOVIES

RUNNING PRESS

ESSAYS
SECTION ONE

Stoner Noir

By Danilo Castro

The first act of Raymond Chandler's novel *The Long Goodbye* (1953) spans months and covertly sets up the plot. Every minor detail has purpose, every conversation insight. It's a chess game in narrative form, considerate of repercussions that only become clear in the finale. The opening of the 1973 film adaptation is a different story. A *very* different story. It spans one night, and sees detective Philip Marlowe (Elliott Gould) stumble around in an attempt to buy cat food. It provides zero exposition, develops none of the secondary characters, and culminates in his cat not even touching the stuff. It's a game of checkers with missing pieces. The spaced-out tone suits the material, but it also makes it easy to miss

the historic context of what's going on. We're witnessing, in essence, the birth of the stoner noir.

Classic film noir is fueled by booze and nicotine, and it has the bleak outcomes and breakneck pacing to prove it. Modern noir has maintained these vices, but its decision to add pot to the mix has expanded the parameters of what a detective story can be. It can be sprawling instead of focused, contemplative instead of emotionally closed off. It can exaggerate tropes to such an absurd degree that they feel subversive. It can also provide lots of dumb fun. Stoner noir is nothing if not self-aware, and seeing licensed professionals arrive at half-baked conclusions is enough to make even the most clueless viewer feel cogent.

Elliott Gould struggled to find work in the year leading up to *The Long Goodbye*. He had developed a reputation for being difficult, but director Robert Altman insisted on casting him and the film revived his career.

These qualities also make stoner noir a difficult style to keep up with. If you aren't careful, you could wind up in a police station with a headache and a questionable drawing in your pocket. Fortunately, we at *NOIR CITY* have assembled a guide to get you through the (reefer) madness. The films discussed here come with symptoms and a correlating stage of highness, so you'll know what to look for and when to watch them in relation to your own trip. Time is of the essence when your perception of time is skewed, so it's best we get started right away.

The Ascent
(symptoms include: bemusement, low energy, impaired depth perception)

Marlowe doesn't explicitly get high in *The Long Goodbye*, but director Robert Altman imbues him with traits that would come to define the stoner detective. He's sleepy, he moves at a snail's pace, and he constantly mumbles. Sure, he smokes like a chimney throughout, but no one would be surprised to learn that he's sampled a few of his neighbor's special brownies behind closed doors. This lack of with-it-ness actually makes him the perfect fall guy when his friend Terry Lennox (Jim Bouton) commits murder and flees to Mexico.

The film's aesthetic choices dull the senses, which is part of what makes it such a perfect gateway viewing. Altman's roaming camera ensures the viewer is constantly off-balance. Most of the pivotal moments are framed through foregrounds that obscure: architecture, foliage, windows. Altman and cinematographer Vilmos Zsigmond "flashed" the film stock with extra light, so whatever visual clues that would've popped out get painted over with a faded, pastel sheen. Nowhere is this more evident than the Wade beach house, where the crashing waves and the reflection of those inside blend into a

One of Altman's friends had a cat who would only eat a specific brand of food. The director worked this humorous occurrence into the film's opening.

Classic Noir

The Motion Picture Production Code allowed very little wiggle room for on-screen drug use in the 1940s. There were essentially two options: exaggerate it as a means of condemnation or downplay it as a low-class vice. Film noir dabbled in both. Take, for example, the inciting murder in *The Big Sleep* (1946). Philip Marlowe (Humphrey Bogart) finds a corpse in a Laurel Canyon house, and the only witness, Carmen Sternwood (Martha Vickers), is too dazed to acknowledge what happened. A slap elicits a non sequitur from Sternwood ("You're cute!") and the private detective responds in surprisingly plain fashion: "You're higher than a kite."

Similarly brief references are baked into films like *Manhandled* (1949) and *Try and Get Me!* (1951). The latter sees a truck driver offer his passenger (Frank Lovejoy) a treat, only to pass it off as a "toothpick" when the passenger looks alarmed. The fact that "toothpick" is slang for a thinly rolled joint all but confirms the subtext. *Manhandled* features Sterling Hayden as an offbeat insurance agent who's constantly changing out of his pajamas. It's a far cry from the grim persona the actor would cultivate in the following decade, but it makes perfect sense when he visits a dispensary and gleefully ingests a cocktail of Benzedrine and downers. Hayden was a recreational user in real life, and this film, coupled with his turn as a suicidal author in *The Long Goodbye*, makes him a rare repeat offender in the stoner noir canon.

Mrs. Vargas (Janet Leigh) runs afoul of the dope-smoking Grandi gang.

Because the noir style made its way into every corner of Hollywood, some propaganda films have a facade of artistic credibility. *She Shoulda Said No!* (1949) was directed by Sam Newfield and stars Lila Leeds, both of whom dabbled in noir proper during the Poverty Row heyday. Their inclusion feels reluctant, however, as Newfield used an alias and Leeds was desperate to rebrand herself after being arrested for drug possession with Robert Mitchum. The rebrand didn't work, and neither does the film. *High School Confidential!* (1958) is another limp attempt at propaganda, with the only highlight being the musical performance by hophead Jerry Lee Lewis.

Touch of Evil (1958) is the most notable film to grapple with pot during this classic period. The protagonist, Miguel Vargas (Charlton Heston), is a drug enforcement agent, so what better way for a border town gang to get back at him than to corner his wife (Janet Leigh) and get her strung out? Orson Welles's twisted masterpiece features a number of memorable flourishes, like the voice taunting Mrs. Vargas through a motel wall ("You know what a Mary Jane is!?") and the murder committed above her semiconscious body, but the film still amplifies stoner behavior to cartoonishly silly effect.

Even with a filmmaker as visionary as Welles at the helm, it was evident that pop culture needed to undergo the sea change of the 1960s before it was ready for marijuana to be properly implemented and explored within the noir landscape.

Jeff Bridges rubbed his knuckles on his eyes before filming scenes in which "The Dude" appeared stoned.

single, distorted image. The director's knack for overlapping dialogue is also deployed masterfully here. So much is heard throughout *The Long Goodbye*, and so little of it is seemingly of consequence, that one can't help but fear Marlowe is listening to the wrong person.

That's the thing, though. Marlowe is so amused by his surroundings that he'll engage with whatever nonsense comes his way. It's okay with him. At one point in the film, while he's being booked at the police station, he makes time to chat with the clerk who sold him the cat food in the opening scene. The film intermittently blows Marlowe's high with bursts of violence, but even these moments are capped with a knowing wink. The detective shoots down Lennox in the final scene, then celebrates by hugging a stranger and dancing to the original 1937 version of Johnny Mercer's "Hooray for Hollywood." (Remember the song choice, by the way. "Hooray for Hollywood" is a sentiment that reverberates, satirically, throughout the rest of these films.) Noir had never been so gleefully irreverent, and the film's ability to both honor and unravel the past ensured it was way ahead of its time. It's the kind of backward logic that only Altman, a legendary pothead himself, could have conjured up.

The Peak

(symptoms include: heightened senses, short attention span, pressured speech)

There's a dude named Jeff Lebowski (Jeff Bridges) who operates on a similar wavelength. Not the millionaire, but the one who literally goes by the moniker "The Dude." He lives in Venice, and if you squint just right, you'd swear he frequents the same grocery chain as Marlowe. He gets attacked by dimwits who soil his rug and demand payment for his wife's gambling debts. The kicker? They meant to accost the *other* Lebowski (David Huddleston); the one with the millions. These are the farcical misunderstandings that fuel *The Big Lebowski* (1998). It's a more exciting film than *The Long Goodbye*, but it's also more intense and scatterbrained, which makes it the perfect stoner noir for the peak stage. There's as much importance put upon helping Lebowski as there is the Dude's bowling tournament or whatever nonsensical debate he might be having with his buddies.

The Big Lebowski has achieved cult status through its comedy, but directors Joel and Ethan Coen

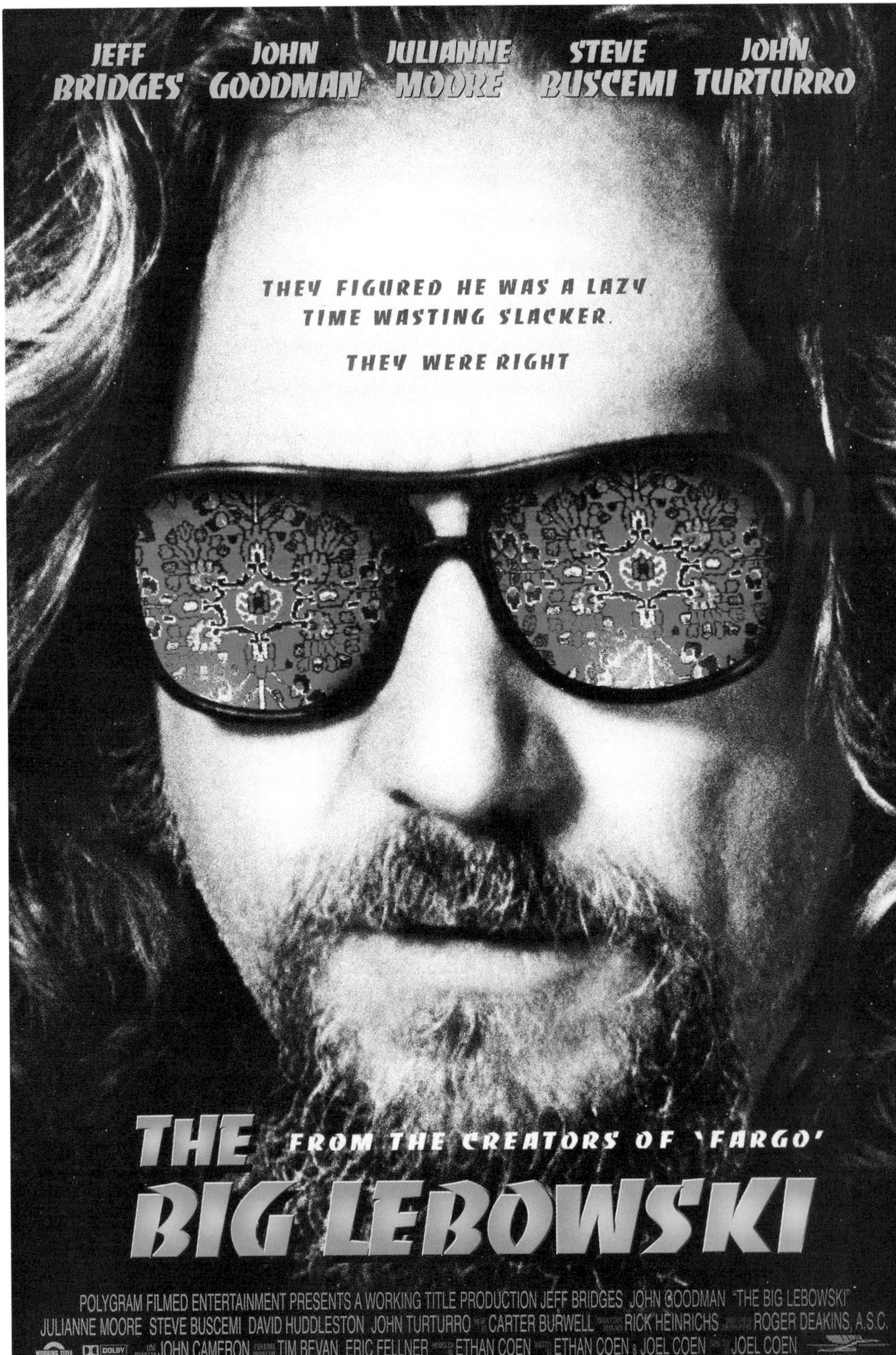

JEFF BRIDGES
JOHN GOODMAN
JULIANNE MOORE
STEVE BUSCEMI
JOHN TURTURRO
THEY FIGURED HE WAS A LAZY TIME WASTING SLACKER.
THEY WERE RIGHT
THE BIG LEBOWSKI
FROM THE CREATORS OF 'FARGO'
POLYGRAM FILMED ENTERTAINMENT PRESENTS A WORKING TITLE PRODUCTION JEFF BRIDGES JOHN GOODMAN "THE BIG LEBOWSKI"
JULIANNE MOORE STEVE BUSCEMI DAVID HUDDLESTON JOHN TURTURRO CARTER BURWELL RICK HEINRICHS ROGER DEAKINS, A.S.C.
JOHN CAMERON TIM BEVAN ERIC FELLNER ETHAN COEN ETHAN COEN & JOEL COEN JOEL COEN
WORKING TITLE
DOLBY
POLYGRAM FILMED ENTERTAINMENT

The voice-over of the Stranger (Sam Elliott, right) was meant to evoke the narration found in Raymond Chandler novels.

have such an intuitive grasp of noir mechanics that they're able to blend the two styles seamlessly. The Dude is a bad detective, as his clothing and skunk odor suggest, so his attempts to play it straight often lead to the film's biggest laughs. The best example of this comes late in the film, when the Dude shades in the indentation of a torn notepad. Instead of an address or crucial phrase, he gets a drawing of a guy with a hard-on. It gets worse when you consider the drawing stays in his pocket during the Busby Berkeley fever dream (the film's undisputed "high" point) and is then found by the cops. Like we said at the onset, don't make the same mistake.

The man behind the hard-on doodle, Jackie Treehorn (Ben Gazzara), is emblematic of the larger role that Hollywood plays in these films. Stoner noir is a phenomenon exclusive to Southern California, and as such, it can be difficult to pin down where the pot smoke ends and the smoke and mirrors begin. Luckily, the inhalation of one allows characters to see right through the other. The Dude is an outsider, which makes him immune to the spoils that someone like Jackie can offer to look the other way. It elicits mockery, sure, but it also makes him the honorable exception in a city where corruption goes unchecked. Porn kings pull the strings, nihilist pop groups set fire to cars, and it all gets swept under the (soiled) rug with a smile.

For all its chaos, *The Big Lebowski* promotes a Zen worldview. The Dude is dealt one setback after another, and he doesn't let it deter from his general demeanor. He's so Zen, in fact, that the final scene breaks down the fourth wall so he can riff with his own narrator, the Stranger (Sam Elliott). Why not, right? When asked to summarize the events of the film, he states, plainly and profoundly, "Ups and downs, strikes and gutters." Fans have theorized as to whether the Dude knows he's being watched, or if the Stranger is some divine entity, but to get hung up on the semantics is to miss the point entirely. We're all just bowling balls in the game of life, man. Abide, like El Duderino, and the pins will fall into place.

Doc's appearance was modeled after a Neil Young photo from 1970. Young's "Journey through the Past" also soundtracks a crucial scene in the film.

The Plateau
(symptoms include: introspection, anxiety, mild hallucinations)

Doc Sportello (Joaquin Phoenix), the hippie shamus from *Inherent Vice* (2014), takes us through the densest part of the trip. He agrees to find a real estate mogul as a favor to his ex-girlfriend, Shasta Fay (Katherine Waterston), and proceeds to unravel a sweater's worth of yarn connecting deranged loan sharks, dentists on trampolines, and a "renaissance cop" who does commercials when he's not guesting on *Adam-12*. Doc does his best to stay professional, but even he loses focus during scenes that play out like stoner Mad Libs. A visit to gonzo dentist Rudy Blatnoyd (Martin Short) results in both men doing coke, before discussing the merits of insanity ("It's not groovy!") and hitching a ride with a teenage girl that Doc rescued years earlier.

Attempts to follow the plot will leave you dazed and confused like Doc, who at one point resorts to drawing names and arrows on his walls. Reading the source novel by Thomas Pynchon will do little to lessen the confusion (the novel was inspired by the film version of *The Long Goodbye*), but it does reveal the crucial change that writer-director Paul Thomas Anderson made in his adaptation. While the novel uses the Shasta Fay breakup as an allegory for the end of the hippie generation, the film inverts this structure so that the hippie fallout serves to underline Doc's heartache. Subtext becomes text, and vice versa. It's a logical choice, given the filmmaker's penchant for trauma-fueled storytelling, and a smart one, as it provides grounded motivation for a mystery that's anything but.

If you're following along, you'll notice introspection coincides with hallucinations that are cleverly woven into the film. The narrator, Sortilège (Joanna Newsom), gives Doc advice yet never talks to anyone else. One scene has her riding shotgun in the detective's car, lamenting L.A.'s changing scenery, only to be absent when he arrives at his destination. Is she an old friend or a side effect of Doc's overworked cerebellum? The same can be asked of Shasta Fay's increasingly bizarre cameos. She exists, but does the version that Doc reunites with exist only in his head? Anderson essentially invites *us* to become the stoned detective, making sense of scenes and dialogue that our protagonist is too compromised to reconcile.

The phrase "inherent vice" refers to items that can't be insured because of their unstable nature. Eggs break, chocolate melts, glass shatters—yet these items pale in comparison to the instability of man, which is what the film is ultimately about. Doc will never get another Summer of Love because his relationship with Shasta Fay, like the world around him, is subject to change. He can either reject it or roll with it. The closing moments see the couple in a different kind of haze; a fog bank, as they drive toward an uncertain future. A white light catches Doc's eye in the rearview mirror, and he grins. We never find out if the light signifies the cops, another hallucination, or even a cherished memory because Doc keeps on rolling. *Inherent Vice* is an esoteric hang, like the high that accompanies it, but these undefined qualities are what make the film so intriguing.

The Descent
(symptoms include: paranoia, lethargy, memory impairment)

If you haven't already noticed, stoner noir is obsessed with the past. Filmmakers love using specific time periods to poke fun at the societal ills that informed their soft-boiled detectives. *Inherent Vice* dips into the post-Manson disillusionment of 1970. *The Big Lebowski* takes place seven years before its release date, in 1991, and while seemingly minor, the distinction is crucial. The film bears the scars of Reaganomics and yuppie culture, right down to the Dude's hatred of the Eagles. *The Long Goodbye*, while technically set during the year it was released, is an inverted period piece, in that Marlowe is depicted as a character who fell asleep in 1953 and woke up two decades later (he was dubbed "Rip Van Marlowe" during filming). Then there's *Under the Silver Lake* (2018), which takes the concept of nostalgia and pushes it to its logical nadir.

The film is set in 2011, when retro-hipster culture reigned supreme and the word "old" had become synonymous with "authentic." Sam (Andrew Garfield) is the heir apparent to Doc and the Dude, but he's so enamored with their respective eras that he somehow gets less done. The brain cells that should be used to stave off eviction are squandered in the company of classic records and posters, obsessively cataloging Vanna White's eyeline on *Wheel of Fortune*. Sam's cloudy existence clears up when he meets Sarah (Riley Keough), but she disappears within hours of their first date, leading the amateur sleuth to make sense of the clues she left behind.

Luckily, *Under the Silver Lake* is loaded with them. The film's writer-director, David Robert Mitch-

Sam (Andrew Garfield) wakes up from a drug-fueled bender in Hollywood Forever Cemetery. Given the film's central themes, the location is particularly fitting.

Even Sam's fantasies are unoriginal. The pool scene parodies Marilyn Monroe's unreleased final film, *Something's Got to Give* (1962).

ell, enlisted the help of cryptologists during preproduction, and the unconventional process resulted in scenes that counteract foreground action with meta-references, audial codes, and visual ciphers. There's breaking the form and then there's methodically dismantling it, which is what occurs here. The film opens with four seemingly random symbols, then provides the translation on a coffee menu minutes later. The score pulls directly from Bernard Herrmann's *Vertigo* (1958) theme, and the only piece of diegetic music spells out the plot in its lyrics. Mitchell is retracing the steps of earlier noir, but he purposefully ditches the fun, as if to impress upon the viewer that the adulation of these films has led to a character and a generation lacking in originality. The burnout, both in terms of this stage of the trip and the Babylonian depiction of the city, is unmistakable.

It's fitting that the stoner noir with the most clues simultaneously provides the least answers. Sam uncovers so many unrelated conspiracies involving Hollywood elites that they render his main quest inert. He loses his girl *and* his apartment in the end, and the only thing he gains is the affirmation that all his idols are false. The catch, of course, is that the film doesn't make clear which of these discoveries carry weight and which are the result of playing one too many records in reverse. Maybe Sam's friend was right when he said: "We crave mystery 'cause there's none left." The character is too far gone to make a ruling, and if you've managed to keep pace, you may be too.

So what does it all mean? What lessons should be gleaned from riding the roller coaster that is stoner noir? Well, for one, detectives who smoke pot *never* seem to get paid. It's a wonder they manage to stay in business. More importantly, though, they differ from their hardboiled counterparts in their even-keeled optimism. These men know that solving a mystery isn't going to resolve the world's problems, and they set their sights on smaller, less tangible victories as a result. Sometimes, reuniting a saxophone player with his family, or forming a genuine bond with another person, is enough. Other times, a really good joint can suffice. The films might be hazy on their own, but the ethos of stoner noir as a whole is strikingly clear: control what you can and shrug off the rest. ■

NO EXIT

HOW FRANZ KAFKA'S DARK FABLE BECAME ORSON WELLES'S MASTERWORK

By Rachel Walther

"It has been said that the logic of this story is the logic of a dream," Orson Welles intones in his introductory narration to *The Trial* (1962). Welles's noir films melted nightmare with reality into a worldview that is both haunting and prescient, presenting a dizzying visual style that helped define the genre. *The Trial* is a grim fantasia that arrests the senses and offers up Welles's bleakest portrayal of society's cruel nature, while proving the enduring allure of sleepwalking through the shadows. Produced in Europe and long lost in obscurity, Welles's most mature noir has now returned to receive the acclaim it is long overdue.

ESCAPE FROM HOLLYWOOD

It was 1961 and Orson Welles was adrift. Since his bitter experience with *Touch of Evil* (1958)—where his exquisite noir creation was chopped up and diluted in the editing room at the behest of Universal Pictures—he'd spent most of his time in Europe, subsisting on a variety of acting roles and theater projects (including a fortnight back in Hollywood to appear as a fictionalized version of Clarence Darrow in the courtroom thriller *Compulsion* [1959]). His efforts to fund a new film, *Chimes at Midnight*, were not materializing. Then, the ragtag father-and-son production team of Michel and Alexander Salkind approached him with a proposition: Would Welles like to do an adaptation of a literary classic? He countered that he much preferred to do an original story of his own, but the Salkinds demurred. They all finally agreed on Franz Kafka's novel *The Trial* (written ca. 1915, published 1925), and Welles spent the next six months hammering out a screenplay. The resulting film would be not only one of the most enjoyable working experiences of the director's career, but also free from producer or studio interference, resulting in the purest expression of his dark vision of the world since *Citizen Kane* (1941). In an interview with *Cahiers du cinéma* a few years after its debut, Welles articulated how special this project was despite its poor showing critically and commercially: "Say what you like, but *The Trial* is the best film I ever made."

Anthony Perkins had also decamped to Europe, enjoying more freedom than he'd known since becoming a promising young star in Hollywood a few years earlier. The dream-factory gauntlet of prying interviews and studio-arranged "dates" with young starlets had exhausted him, but his homosexuality, a serious liability in Hollywood, caused barely a ripple in Europe. *Psycho* (1960) had debuted in the United States to massive acclaim—his role as nervous, charming, homicidal innkeeper Norman Bates was the finest performance of his career—and in return he'd been snubbed at the Oscars and his very presence now frightened people on the streets. The high-strung, temperamental actor had unfortunately been "typecast as himself," in the words of Perkins biographer Charles Winecoff. But in the spring of 1962, the *Psycho* cement had yet

Both Welles and Anthony Perkins (right, with costar Jeanne Moreau) decamped to Europe for more freedom, both personally and professionally.

ANCESTOR AND OUTLIER: KAFKA'S WORLD ON FILM

In many ways, the themes of Franz Kafka's novels and short stories—not to mention his heartrending and gloomy biography—serve as a recipe for noir: unseen persecution, omniscient surveillance, seductive and deceptive women, endings full of ambivalence and despair. Yet adaptations of his work have remained exclusively art house and decidedly un-noir. Why?

In Kafka's work, truths are unknowable and irrelevant ("We needn't accept everything as true—only as necessary"), and good and evil are valueless foreign currencies. His is a world where noir attitudes were adopted so long ago, they've given way to amnesiac complacency. The tension between a societal definition of justice and the character's actions—which fuels much of the excitement in noir stories—is absent. This may explain why his work has remained elusive for noir audiences, but why it's rewarding to look back on as a source of continued inspiration.

Michael Haneke's *The Castle* (1997), based on Kafka's final, unfinished novel, pounces on the book's elements of dominance and brutality (two favorite themes for both the author and the director) to present a story that's viscous in tone and drab in appearance. Welles's time-out-of-time technique is evident with characters adopting contemporary late-1990s clothing and hairstyles while utilizing mid-century telephones and horse-drawn sleighs. Land Surveyor K (Ulrich Mühe) is embroiled in an increasingly frustrating attempt to receive his work duties from the Castle and make connections with townspeople who can grant him access to his superiors. But K never reaches the Castle and Haneke never even allows us to see it, keeping the framing tight in on the characters, with no establishing shots or locations shown in full. This casts a spell that is decidedly more absurd than noir, portraying cruelty as an action of incessant tedium rather than one of chiaroscuro terror. In director Rudolf Noelte's earlier version of the same novel (*Das Schloss* [1968]), Maximilian Schell stars as K and the action is presented in a more straightforward manner, but the result reads more as an allegory for Soviet-era surveillance and persecution than as a timeless echo of society's inhumane proclivities.

The 1993 BBC production of *The Trial* has a great pedigree: screenplay by Harold Pinter, with Kyle MacLachlan starring as Josef K in a cast that also includes Jason Robards, Anthony Hopkins, and David Thewlis. But in hewing closer to Kafka's novel, the unfinished reality of the text becomes more apparent. MacLachlan's version of K is so imperious and unsympathetic, and the action so staid and illogical, that the adaptation is neither absurd nor noir, just a dry exercise in pithy confusion.

Rather than adapting a single work, screenwriter Lem Dobbs blended aspects from a number of Kafka's stories along with details from the author's biography—and a dash of murder and horror—to fashion *Kafka* (1991), directed by Steven Soderbergh and starring Jeremy Irons as the eponymous hero. And hero he is: humble insurance clerk by day, visionary writer at night. Shot in black and white and set in mid-1910s Prague, the film follows Kafka as he is snapped out of his humdrum existence when a colleague disappears under mysterious circumstances. In his attempt to find his friend, the would-be writer gets ensnared in a fantastic web of police corruption, terrorist cells, and homicidal manimals. A grab bag of influences—from Welles's *The Trial* to F. W. Murnau, *Island of Lost Souls* (1932), and *Brazil* (1985)—pepper the visuals and steer the plot, and the result is a fun homage to the author that's successful as a noir, since it offers a modicum of redemption, even if only as an unattainable prize.

to set over in Europe, and Perkins was Welles's only choice to play Josef K, protagonist in *The Trial* and Kafka's alter ego.

A BEAUTIFUL NIGHTMARE

Kafka's story is a dizzying maze of bureaucratic tedium and malignant indifference. It begins the morning Josef K, a senior bank clerk, is roused from a sound sleep and told he is under arrest. The charges are serious but unnamed, and for the time being he can go about his business as usual. But the specter of guilt casts a pall over his life, and in an effort to learn more about the charges and clear himself, he's drawn into a surreal world of suspicion, innuendo, and self-doubt. Has K perhaps committed a crime that he can't recall? Is there something in his very nature that sets him apart from the rest of society, something he must be punished for? "It's even worse when you haven't done anything wrong and you still feel guilty," he broods. Eventually K's fate is decided, and he is ruthlessly dispatched by the very system he served faithfully.

The other pivotal role in the novel is that of K's lawyer (renamed Hastler in Welles's film). Hastler is both K's advocate and his by-proxy persecutor, a stand-in for the unseen, accusatory forces of the judicial system. Hastler is confident in his ability to manage K's case, while arrogantly admitting the danger of exonerating his client: "To be in chains is sometimes safer than to be free." Welles had initially hoped to cast Charles Laughton as the imposing figure, and Jackie Gleason was also considered, but eventually Welles took the role himself, later quipping: "I was the only actor of my caliber that I could afford." After exteriors were filmed in Zagreb, the Salkinds ran short on funds and Welles was forced to scrap the construction of his planned interiors. Nothing short of a miracle was required—a

Kafka's bureaucratic tedium brought to life; Perkins was Welles's only choice to play Josef K, the persecuted bank clerk.

The Gare d'Orsay station was a dream location that infused the film with a timeless surrealism.

dream location that could enhance the confusion of Kafka's story while sating the director's appetite for dynamic low angles and complete control of lighting conditions. The disused Gare d'Orsay train station in Paris—a cavernous rabbit warren of dilapidated rooms filled with just the type of decaying, administrative madness required—was available and became another character in the film. Its zigzag of visually stunning hallways, anterooms, and grand halls built in 1900 in the Beaux-Arts style, combined with the actors' modern clothes and dialogue, placed the action in a world of its own, familiar but just out of step with contemporary life.

Rounding out the cast is a trio of women, playing characters who alternately bewitch, distract, or dissuade K from pursuing his case: Jeanne Moreau (as Frau Burstner, K's neighbor), Romy Schneider (as Leni, Hastler's nursemaid), and Elsa Martinelli (as Hilda, the wife of a court functionary). Akim Tamiroff plays Bloch, a long-term client of Hastler's who slavishly accepts his lawyer's dismissive and abusive treatment. Welles leveraged the differing scales of his myriad locations to display Perkins at a variety of sizes: in a Zagreb apartment block, he's scraping his head against the ceiling of his claustrophobic rooming house, while in a scene shot in a massive room of the Gare d'Orsay, his six-foot-two frame can barely reach the handles of the massive double doors. All sound in the film was dubbed in postproduction to save money, and Welles provided the voices of many of the supporting cast himself. This was a technique he'd employed before, most notably in his globetrotting adventure *Mr. Arkadin* (aka *Confidential Report*, 1955). This disembodiment of sound and disorientation of scale, layered with the haunting refrain of Tomaso Albinoni's *Adagio in G Minor*, is stitched together with the variety of classic and modern spaces to create an indefinite world that's a bleak and stunning European nowheresville. This adds to the hopeless disorientation of Perkins's K—how can he fight for redemption and clear his name when he's not even sure where he is or who is speaking?

For Perkins, *The Trial* was an opportunity to synthesize the carefree energy of his earliest films with the withdrawn, mercurial side he'd displayed in *Psycho*. His Josef K is a mature man who's equal parts appealing, defiant, apprehensive, and doomed. The actor later recalled in an interview: "It was a great experience. . . . I owed myself that. I would have done anything for the experience of working with Orson Welles." It would be the last time the actor collaborated with a director of such prestige (although he did reunite with Welles as an actor in Claude Chabrol's uneven *Ten Days' Wonder* [1971]), and in the following decade he continued to hone darker versions of his persona, most notably in the startling thriller *Pretty Poison* (1968) and the sobering Los Angeles tone poem *Play It as It Lays* (1972).

OBSCURITY AND RESURRECTION

When *The Trial* debuted in December 1962, the reception was mixed with most critics praising its visual elements while panning the story, the casting, and the pacing. It fell into obscurity and the purgatory of public domain, appearing in countless cheap VHS and DVD versions whose washed-out visuals ironically sapped its most redeeming feature. Even many Welles biographers discount the film: Joseph McBride concludes that *The Trial* is a "striking but strained film that succeeds only intermittently," and in his multivolume biography, Simon Callow proclaims it "a problematic film in his output." A new 4K restoration currently touring with Rialto Pictures will go a long way to reassert its power and independence as both a lost art-house treasure and a rare Welles film that does not require a restorative edit or explanatory notes.

Welles was initially lukewarm about depicting Kafka's fatalist view of society. Kafka's Josef K was, for him, too passive, too accepting of the system scheming for his destruction, which Welles viewed as a perspective specific to Kafka's experiences as a Jew in pre–World War I Prague: "There's every possible difference between us. We could not possibly have the same vision." His postwar K could not and would not be the same kind of man, not after the horrors of the Holocaust. As Welles adjusted K's temperament to suit a modern protagonist, he sacrificed a key tenet of Kafka's novel in order to serve a greater cinematic purpose. Unlike the novel's K—who unwittingly participates in his own persecution with his priggish demeanor and zest for authority—Perkins's K is defiant and curious. He is now guilty of something tangible: asking questions with dangerous answers. It is due to this new, challenging attitude that *The Trial*'s Kafkaesque gloom shifts to righteous Wellesian indignation. Like Guy Van Stratten in *Mr. Arkadin* (1955), Mike Vargas in *Touch of Evil*, and Michael O'Hara in *The Lady from Shanghai* (1948), this Josef K is a young man snared in a web of manipulation who attempts to unmask the powerful men pulling the strings and regain his freedom.

In often casting himself as the antagonist to these heroes and portraying them as imposing yet compelling figures surrounded by sycophants and lovely women, Welles drew attention to the complex network of those who benefit from a corrupt system, and the high price paid in fighting for one more just. His Josef K becomes another stand-in for Welles himself, who had been losing every battle since 1942 but was still fighting. Here, in an abandoned train station half a world away from Hollywood, he finally won a round, creating (and completing) an exquisite and wholly unique creative vision—one that will now hopefully take its rightful place in the top tier of his peerless career. ∎

ARCHITECTS OF
The Art Directors

ILLUSION

By Jake Hinkson

In the opening scenes of *Murder, My Sweet* (1944), we find private eye Philip Marlowe alone in his shabby little office late at night. A location as iconic to noir fans as the Batcave is to comic book geeks, Marlowe's digs are the perfect expression of the detective's dogged integrity. The battered desk under a bank of grimy windows. Blinking neon signs for Chinese food reflected on the glass. A view of cluttered rooftops and a cheap hotel. The office is humble, the movie seems to be telling us, because the man occupying it isn't for sale at any price.

Because his office so perfectly captures his character, it is a good place to begin discussing one of the most woefully overlooked aspects of film noir: art direction. *Murder, My Sweet* was one of the seminal films of 1944, the year that established so much of what we mean when we use the phrase *film noir*, but while tributes abound to the directors and cinematographers of noir's Golden Age, many scholars and fans alike have often neglected the contributions of the studio art director. Yet these unsung craftsmen were as responsible as anyone for the genre's distinctive visual flair.

Drawing on a knowledge of architecture, scenic design, and interior decoration, the art director would lay out and oversee construction of the physical environment of a film, sometimes before a director was even assigned to a project. As important as they were to any movie production, the influence art directors had on the visual style of classic noir was especially profound. Working hand in hand with a film's producer and cinematographer, art directors didn't just help to shape the look and feel of an individual project, they helped define a new movement—that sprawling collection of disparate movies that we would come to know as film noir.

The Big Three: D'Agostino, Wheeler, and Dreier

The key figure overseeing operations in virtually every studio's art department was the supervising art director. Working beneath him were the unit art directors and assistant art directors he assigned to individual productions. Filling out the staff of each art department were dozens of architects,

Van Nest Polglase created expressionist sets for *Stranger on the Third Floor*, with an assist from Albert D'Agostino (inset).

sketch artists, set decorators, production illustrators, model/miniature makers, and more. For each film being produced by the studio, the art directors managed the efforts of these staffers and coordinated with the research, construction, and property departments[1] in the manufacture of a film's sets and the scouting of locations. In this hierarchical system, the supervising art director could, and often did, establish a house style for their studio.

Just consider the impact of the incomparable **Albert D'Agostino**. At RKO in the 1940s and 1950s, D'Agostino supervised work on virtually every film noir the studio released from *Journey into Fear* in 1943 to *The Unholy Wife* in 1957. And RKO made *dozens* of noirs, more than any other studio. The unifying characteristics of the RKO noir—evocative sets grounded in a realist aesthetic but shaded with moody touches of expressionism—are directly attributable to the supervising art director who oversaw work on all these films. You cannot have a serious conversation about who "invented" film noir without discussing Albert D'Agostino.

Two by D'Agostino and unit art director Jack Okey (inset). Top: *The Set-Up*; Bottom: *Out of the Past*.

After studying architecture and mechanical design at Columbia University and the Mechanics Institute, D'Agostino became a scenic designer for theater productions in 1915, then started designing films for MGM and Lewis Selznick in New York in the 1920s. He joined Universal as a unit art director and relocated to Hollywood in 1925. During D'Agostino's time at the studio, Universal's art department was defined by **Charles D. Hall**'s neo-Gothic designs for films like *Dracula* (1931), *Frankenstein* (1931), and *The Black Cat* (1934). These were clearly an influence on D'Agostino when he designed his own Gothic productions in the 1930s such as *Mystery of Edwin Drood* (1935) and *Werewolf of London* (1935), and he would take this influence with him when he moved to RKO in 1940 and began working on both producer Val Lewton's horror cycle and the emerging genre of noir.[2]

---

1 At some studios, one or more of these departments might actually be a division of the art department.
2 D'Agostino's first noir assignment at RKO, as associate art director, was on the most expressionistic noir of the 1940s, *Stranger on the Third Floor* (1940), under the supervision of Van Nest Polglase.

Lyle Wheeler, supervising art director at 20th Century-Fox, was known as "the dean of Hollywood art directors."

Working directly under a supervising art director like D'Agostino were the unit art directors he assigned to individual films. Most of the hands-on work for an individual film was done by these unit art directors, who cleared their ideas with the supervisor and then worked out the specifics of how a physical environment (sets and set dressing) would look and function within the frame. Given the distinctive darkness of the genre, those specifics were particularly challenging in noir. As the writer David Landau notes in his book *Film Noir Production* (2016), "especially for film noir, the art director had to understand how colors, textures and patterns would read on black-and-white film. Color provides the eye with natural contrast. But once color is removed, everything turns into a shade of gray. How these shades play off each other, creating contrast and texture, is a particular skill of the Hollywood art director." At RKO, D'Agostino had a deep bench of go-to unit art directors who helped him build Dark City, including the brilliant likes of **Jack Okey** (*Out of the Past*, *The Set-Up*, *The Narrow Margin*), **Ralph Berger** (*Armored Car Robbery*, *Where Danger Lives*, *On Dangerous Ground*), and **Walter Keller**[3] (*Born to Kill*, *Desperate*, and *Roadblock*).

One of the most talented art directors in D'Agostino's department was **Carroll Clark**. Clark had been at the studio since 1930, predating D'Agostino himself, when RKO was still known for Art Deco opulence during the legendary run of supervising art director **Van Nest Polglase**. With the coming of D'Agostino and the ascension of noir, the studio's priorities changed, and Clark proved an excellent fit for the new, darker material. He was the art director on films like *Cornered* (1945), *Strange Bargain* (1949), *Clash by Night*

---

3 Walter Keller also did the unit art direction on virtually all of Lewton's films during this same period.

Gene Tierney and Dana Andrews in *Laura*.

(1952), *Angel Face* (1952), *While the City Sleeps* (1956), and *Beyond a Reasonable Doubt* (1956), among others.

It was Clark who collaborated with D'Agostino on *Murder, My Sweet*. On this film, coming in noir's breakthrough year of 1944, they established the quintessential look of the private eye's world.[4] Every setting in the film has its own unique character, and these settings are a study in contrasts—from Marlowe's well-worn office to the run-down home of alcoholic Jessie Florian, from the opulent Rococo mansion inhabited by the millionaire Grayles to the sleek Art Deco digs of dandy Jules Amthor. Working in tandem with

The high-society settings for *Laura* achieved by Lyle Wheeler and unit art director Leland Fuller. Note the original (rejected) portrait of Laura.

the cinematographer, Harry J. Wild, the art directors helped shape the photography and lighting on the film as well. For instance, in one early shot Marlowe and Moose Malloy climb the steps to an upstairs bar, and the camera is positioned low on the street, looking up through the double doors, to capture the angle at which the narrow stairs converge at a point like something out of *The Cabinet of Doctor Caligari* (1920). Likewise, the hallway outside of Marlowe's office, with its angular ceiling and open

---

4   With all due respect to the excellent work done at Warner Bros. by Robert Haas on *The Maltese Falcon* (1941) and Carl Jules Weyl on *The Big Sleep* (1946), it is *Murder, My Sweet* that most evocatively captures the shadowy, hungover world of the classic private eye.

Leave Her to Heaven: Lyle Wheeler and unit art director Maurice Ransford proved that even a bucolic cottage could be the setting for a film noir.

elevator cages, goes a long way toward dictating the cross-sectioning of the shadows. It is this vital interplay of art direction and cinematography that creates the noir aesthetic.

THE MAN DUBBED "the dean of Hollywood art directors" was 20th Century-Fox's **Lyle Wheeler**. After studying architectural design at the University of Southern California, Wheeler worked as an industrial designer and magazine illustrator before being discovered by MGM's Cedric Gibbons in 1929. He rose fast at MGM, but he left in 1936 to go work for David O. Selznick, winning an Oscar for his art direction on *Gone with the Wind* (1939). In 1944, he became the supervising art director at 20th Century-Fox and shaped that studio's productions for the next two decades.[5] As Wheeler told Beverly Heisner in her book *Hollywood Art: Art Direction in the Days of the Great Studios* (1990), "I would scout locations with the art director assigned to each picture, approve all sketches, and most importantly, work with the writer almost from the beginning of the project." Virtually all of 20th Century-Fox's noir output during the classic era was overseen by Wheeler, and his influence on the genre is almost as deep as D'Agostino's.

In 1944, the same year D'Agostino and Clark were making *Murder, My Sweet*, Wheeler and unit art director **Leland Fuller** (*Fallen Angel, Whirlpool, Kiss of Death*) made their own genre-defining film, *Laura*. Unlike the Marlowe adaptation, however, *Laura* is set almost exclusively in the world of high society. The film opens in sophisticate Waldo Lydecker's posh penthouse, complete with a collection of Oriental art, shuttered windows, and views to a terrace beyond. Book-lined walls, antique masks, an ornate grandfather clock, a marbled bathroom, a marble tub with movable desk—the place is the epitome of mid-1940s style.[6] This serves as a subtle contrast with the film's more down-to-earth title character. As Heisner notes:

> Laura's apartment, more intimate than others in the film, is broken up into small interrelated spatial units. . . . The decorative style of the apartment changes from room to room, expressive of Laura's own search for definition. The study is done unexpectedly in a Victorian style, down to Belser sofas, and other action takes place in Laura's bedroom, which is decked in gauzy curtains and has a canopied four-poster bed.

Six years later, Wheeler and unit art director **J. Russell Spencer** (*Nightmare Alley*) designed very different environments for the reteaming of *Laura*'s romantic duo in the bad-cop drama *Where the Sidewalk Ends* (1950). This time Gene Tierney and Dana Andrews would fall in love in cheap boarding rooms with peeling wallpaper and the brick-and-wire confines of a police station.

Wheeler always loved a good set-piece location, an oversized hub for action and character to revolve around. His masterpiece with unit art director **Maurice Ransford** (*Hangover Square, Leave Her to Heaven, Somewhere in the Night*) is the titular beer joint in *Road House* (1948). A sprawling hodgepodge on the Canadian border owned by Jefty Robbins, Jefty's Road House is a magnificent creation—part redneck saloon, part glitzy cocktail lounge, part rustic hunting lodge, part sporting goods store. There are slanted floor-to-ceiling walls of plate glass separating the sections of the club, exposed oak beams in the ceiling, and massive stone fireplaces festooned with antlers and taxidermy. In the basement, there's a ten-lane bowling alley, and upstairs there's a spacious apartment for the establishment's

---

5 Wheeler's predecessor at 20th Century-Fox was Richard Day, who went on leave in 1942 to serve in the Marines for the duration of World War II. Although Day didn't officially leave the studio for good until 1947, most accounts support Wheeler's contention that he was serving as supervising art director as early as 1944.

6 The furnishings, art, and other key touches were provided by *Laura*'s set decorators Thomas Little and Paul S. Fox. It goes without saying that studio set decorators deserve their own extended appreciation.

manager, Pete Morgan. Neon signs adorn every doorway, and the blazing billboard over the joint's main entrance announcing JEFTY'S ROAD HOUSE is almost as big as the building itself.

The size and scope of the *Road House* set is typical of 20th Century-Fox in this period. While other studios were constricting and cutting corners after the war, they were expanding, literally. In the 1950s, the studio would go all in on CinemaScope, and since the silver screen and the pictures shown on them were getting bigger and bigger, so too would the sets. In 1952, Wheeler oversaw construction of a mammoth backlot waterway to be used in as many productions as possible going forward. According to 20th Century-Fox art director Herman Blumenthal, "Preliminary plans for such a scheme had been studied by Wheeler for many years, and progress had been made through permanent landscape planting on a fifteen acre site at the Beverly Hills Studio." This waterway would come in useful for another of Wheeler's signature set pieces.

Two set pieces by Wheeler. Top: *Road House* (with unit art director Maurice Ransford); Bottom: *Pickup on South Street* (with unit art director George Patrick).

For director Sam Fuller's *Pickup on South Street* (1953), Wheeler and unit art director **George Patrick** created a waterfront hideout for the film's amoral antihero, Skip McCoy. Not as tackily grandiose as Jefty's Road House, Skip's little shack under the Brooklyn Bridge is, nonetheless, an iconic location in film noir. It's a barren hovel that evinces no interest by its owner in anything other than the contemplation of criminal enterprise, a floating lair for a penniless pickpocket with a nice view of the bridge and a handy winch and pulley rig to keep his brew cold and his loot stashed. Skip steals, dunks his plunder in the East River, guzzles a beer, catches a nap, and then stalks back out to the sweaty subways to prey again. His hideout, as conceived by Fuller and realized by Wheeler and Patrick, is the perfect expression of his character.

ALONGSIDE D'AGOSTINO at RKO and Wheeler at 20th Century-Fox, rounding out the big three supervising art directors of noir's classic age was **Hans Dreier** at Paramount. Born in Germany in 1885, Dreier studied architecture in Munich and worked for the German government in West Africa. After World War I, he began working in movies in Berlin before being scouted by Paramount

Alan Ladd gets the drop on Veronica Lake in Paramount's *This Gun for Hire* on grimy sets courtesy of supervising art director Hans Dreier (below) and unit art director Robert Usher.

in 1923. Another long timer, he stayed at his home studio until he retired in 1950. In the thirties, he was instrumental in shaping Paramount's air of European sophistication. A favorite of both Ernst Lubitsch and Josef von Sternberg, he was capable of creating anything those vastly different directors needed—from the elegant Parisian settings of Lubitsch's *Trouble in Paradise* (1932) to the grotesque expressionism of Sternberg's *The Scarlet Empress* (1934).

When noir came along in the forties, Dreier was there to infuse it with Germanic mood. His work on Sternberg crime pictures like *Underworld* (1927) and *The Docks of New York* (1928) had paved the way for the hardboiled urbanism he would bring to bear on early noirs like *This Gun for Hire* (1942, with **Robert Usher**), *Street of Chance* (1942, with **Haldane Douglas**), and *The Glass Key* (1942, with Haldane Douglas). More than D'Agostino or Wheeler, Dreier also continued to take a hand in the actual day-to-day design work on individual films, sketching designs at his drawing board in ink and charcoal. More than any other supervising art director, Dreier's films had a personal touch.

Which isn't to say that he didn't also utilize the talent in his department. One unit art director who worked for him, **Boris Leven**, remembered that Dreier ran the department with military efficiency. "Every morning Dreier would walk through the entire department, stopping at each desk, making comments on your sketches or on the film in preproduction." In addition to Leven, Dreier's roster of unit art directors at Paramount included **Franz Bachelin** (*I Walk Alone, Night Has a Thousand Eyes, Alias Nick Beal, Dark City*), **Earl Hedrick** (*The Accused; Sorry, Wrong Number; Union Station; Detective Story*), and **John Meehan** (*The Strange Love of Martha Ivers, Sunset Boulevard*).

During this time, his key art director in the unit, and the man who would eventually succeed Dreier

Dreier and unit art director Hal Pereira helped create the noir style with *Double Indemnity*.

when he retired, was **Hal Pereira** (*Ministry of Fear, Ace in the Hole, Detective Story*). Born in 1905, Pereira started out as an architect before coming to work at Paramount as an illustrator. Recognizing his talent, Dreier took Pereira under his wing. One of Pereira's first assignments as an art director would prove to be *the* genre-defining film noir of 1944.

With *Double Indemnity*, Dreier and Pereira forever established the cinematic presence of Los Angeles as distinctly, almost inherently, noir. Phyllis Dietrichson's hacienda, a Spanish Colonial Revival with red clay tile rooftops and thick white stucco walls, is one of the genre's signature locations, a place oozing casual material wealth and bored bourgeois comfort.[7] Inside, the place is dark, like a great gray cave baking in the sun, with light slipping in through the wooden slats of the venetian blinds. Later, when Phyllis and her lover Walter Neff meet up to plan how to murder her husband, *Double Indemnity* turns the supermarket grocery store—the very symbol of 1940s American consumerism—into the epicenter of lawlessness. The couple does their scheming among wide, anonymous aisles and geometrically precise pyramids of soup cans, beneath signs urging shoppers to get MORE FOR LESS.[8]

From Culver City to Poverty Row: Studio Stalwarts and Free Agents

By far the most famous art director in the Golden Age of Hollywood was **Cedric Gibbons**, who was appointed supervising art director at MGM shortly after the studio was formed in 1924 and stayed there

---

[7] The Dietrichson home, like many noir settings, is a blend of carefully chosen exterior locations and well-constructed interior studio sets. It was part of the art director's job to design the seamless flow of one into another.

[8] *Double Indemnity* also has one of noir's nuttiest designs: the door of Neff's apartment, which inexplicably opens outward *into* the hallway for no reason other than to give Phyllis something to hide behind when the lovers are surprised by Neff's boss, Barton Keyes—a scene not in the original source novel, and a clear example of the script dictating the set design.

the rest of his career. While most art directors, even the supervisors, were largely unheralded craftsmen, Gibbons was an outsized figure in the industry. In addition to having his name on some 1,500 films and winning *eleven* Oscars (he also designed the Oscar statue itself), he was married to a movie star, Dolores del Rio. Most importantly, he ran the largest, most well-funded art department in Hollywood.

But MGM only dabbled in noir, often to mixed results. The difference between most MGM noirs under Gibbons's administration and those made further down the economic ladder wasn't just money, it was pretension. MGM studio chief Louis B. Mayer hated "realism" as an aesthetic and he demanded to see a film's budget on the screen. Thus, something like MGM's *The Postman Always Rings Twice* (1946) looks uncommonly neat and clean, even pretty, because while Mayer might reluctantly consent to produce an adaptation of James M. Cain's trashy potboiler, he wasn't about to let Gibbons and unit art director **Randall Duell** make it look *cheap* to boot.⁹

Compare *The Postman Always Rings Twice* to something like *Detour*, made by the Poverty Row studio Producers Releasing Corporation in 1945. Here, art director **Edward Jewell**'s sets look like they've been cobbled together out of discount toilet paper and bounced checks. Before the lead actor even opens his mouth, *Detour* reeks of desperation and tough luck. It looks cheap, in other words, because it is cheap. PRC couldn't pull off a neat and pretty production if it had to, so Jewell leaned into the tawdriness of it all. And that was perfect. His sets—so threadbare and spare they almost seem avant-garde—provide the crucial physical context for the film's minimalist intensity. This helps explain why *Detour* is a far better example of film noir than *The Postman Always Rings Twice*. After all, the whole point of an MGM movie was to let the viewer bask in the glamor of money-is-no-consideration production values. PRC, on the other hand, had no glamor to sell. At PRC, money (or the lack of it) was *always* a consideration, making the studio the ideal place to produce a movie about people struggling to survive on society's economic margins.

EVERY STUDIO IN HOLLYWOOD had its key art directors, and most studios knew whom to entrust with a film noir. At Universal, **John B. Goodman** served as supervising art director during the pivotal years of 1943–46, during which time he worked on early Robert Siodmak noirs like *Phantom Lady* (1944), *Christmas Holiday* (1944), and *The Suspect* (1944). **Alexander Golitzen** took over as supervisor in the fifties after amassing credits that included Fritz Lang's *Scarlet Street* (1945). Among his most talented unit art directors was **Robert Clatworthy** (who had shared credits with Goodman on *Phantom Lady* and *Christmas Holiday*), and together Golitzen and Clatworthy did the art direction on Orson Welles's final studio film, *Touch of Evil* (1958), seen by some scholars as the culmination of the original noir cycle.

Warner Bros. didn't have an all-powerful supervising art director in the mold of the other major studios, but its noir output was distinguished by the work of its two most respected art directors: **Anton Grot** (*Mildred Pierce, The Unsuspected, The Two Mrs. Carrolls*) and **Carl Jules Weyl** (*The Big Sleep, Out of the Fog, The Letter*).¹⁰ Important work in noir was also done by Warner Bros. stalwarts like **Charles H. Clarke** (*Dark Passage, Caged, Tomorrow Is Another Day*) and **Edward Carrere** (*White Heat, The Breaking Point, Dial M for Murder*).

Of course, not every talented art director was a company man who stayed at one studio his entire career. Consider the career of poverty-row drifter **Frank Paul Sylos**, a Brooklyn-born Yale-trained illustrator who seemingly worked for every fly-by-night production company in town, a partial list of which would include everyone from the enterprising King Brothers to W. Lee Wilder (Billy Wilder's estranged brother), as well as a regular gig for Pine-Thomas Productions. Sylos may have stayed a free agent, but he worked on some of the best noirs made on Poverty Row, including *When Strangers Marry* (1944,

---

9   When Dore Schary was appointed head of production at MGM in 1948, ending Mayer's era of absolute control, he greenlit more noirs and let the art directors pursue a realist aesthetic. In 1950, Gibbons and Duell delivered *The Asphalt Jungle*, which looks, at times, like American neorealism. Louis B. Mayer loathed the film.
10 Although **Bertram Tuttle** did uncredited work as supervisor, Warner Bros. has fewer split-credits among its art directors than other studios. Without a powerful supervising art director to claim co-credit on every production, it's remarkably easier to say who did what on an individual picture.

MGM's dashing supervising art director Cedric Gibbons with his wife, movie star Dolores del Río.

for the King Brothers), *Fear* (1946, at Monogram), and *99 River Street* (1953, for Edward Small Productions). All he had to work with on some of these productions was loose change and sweat, but he knew how to stretch a nickel as well as anyone, and when low-rent PRC got bought out by the British production company Eagle-Lion Films and made a run at producing a quality feature with *Ruthless* (1948), they turned to Sylos to make it happen. The result was a poverty-row *Citizen Kane* that was sadly butchered in the editing room but nevertheless has a confident, handsome physical production.

The most consequential independent art director was undoubtedly **William Cameron Menzies**. A legendary figure whose career stretched back to the early days of cinema,[11] he played such an important role in the design of films at Selznick International, including the mammoth *Gone with the Wind*, that he was given the title "production designer." Over time, the term caught on and the role of art director would eventually become subordinate to the more empowered position of production designer. In 2012, the Academy

Top: Warner Bros. unit art director Anton Grot; Bottom: Grot's work on *Mildred Pierce* (with uncredited work by Bertram Tuttle).

of Motion Picture Arts and Sciences formalized this shift by changing the "Award for Best Art Direction" to the "Award for Best Production Design."

Still, when we look back at classic noir, we have to stop and take stock of the incredible accomplishments of all those Golden Age art directors working behind the scenes. They constructed every hideout, flophouse, dive bar, police precinct, and glitzy nightclub we love to remember. Whether they ever picked up an Oscar statue, or they spent their entire careers toiling away in relative obscurity at their drawing boards, these largely forgotten artists were the urban planners of Dark City. When we slip into the dreamworld of film noir all these years later, we're entering a world that they built. ■

---

11   Menzies was, in fact, the winner of the first Academy Award for art direction for *The Dove* (1927).

THE NAKED EYE
REALISM AND THE TRUE CRIME AESTHETIC

By Imogen Sara Smith

Since the invention of cinema, movies have fed two contradictory yet entangled desires: for fact and fantasy, truth and magic, realism and escape. Cinema began with the *actualités* of the Lumière brothers, which documented real people, real streets, real trains; and the *féeries* of Georges Méliès, which harnessed the camera's ability to visualize the impossible and the fantastic. These approaches seem like stark opposites, but every film has aspects of both. Even the most scrupulous cinéma verité transforms its subject with framing and editing; even the most stylized Hollywood musical is a record of something that happened in front of a camera.

Film noir is associated with expressionistic stylization and the artifice of Hollywood studio filmmaking, but also with "gritty realism." After World War II, crime dramas were at the forefront of a movement to bring documentary elements into the dream factory—location shooting, natural lighting, and narratives based on fact. But the relationship between a realist aesthetic and true crime stories goes back much further, encompassing a host of visual influences and techniques in the quest for veracity. Here are three examples of the dissenting strain that has always pushed against the movies' preference for beautiful make-believe.

How the Other Half Lives: *Regeneration* (1915)

Considered the first full-length gangster movie, *Regeneration* was based on *My Mamie Rose* (1903), the colorful autobiography of Owen Frawley Kildare, a self-described "beer slinger and pugilist in a tough Bowery dive." Kildare (the name may have been a pseudonym) recounted growing up as an abused orphan on the Lower East Side and running with a street gang until his life was transformed by a woman who worked at a local settlement house, who taught him to read and encouraged his early efforts at writing. The popular book was a tribute to this savior, who tragically died of pneumonia a week before they were to be married. A stage adaptation in 1908 gave the story a punchier ending where the saintly woman is killed by a gangster's bullet, and Owen bears responsibility for ensnaring her in his old life. Kildare's dismay at this twisting of the facts seems to have contributed to a mental breakdown, and by the time Raoul Walsh (with co-writer Carl Harbaugh) turned the play into a movie, retaining this violent climax, the author had died in a state hospital.

Regeneration, Walsh's directorial debut after working as an actor and assistant to D. W. Griffith, was a hit with both critics and audiences, solidly establishing his career. He shot the film in New York, recruiting real street characters—hoodlums, prostitutes, Bowery bums—as extras. (According to legend, Griffith had used real gangsters in his 1912 short film *The Musketeers of Pig Alley*.) Walsh had grown up in Manhattan, but in a privileged setting closer to that of the uptown swells in the film who come down to the Bowery on a slumming trip. He went hog-wild playing up the squalor of the slums, packing the film with grotesquely disfigured faces and disabled or obese bodies. In the tenements, young Owen grows up surrounded by cracked and peeling walls, shredded curtains, broken chairs, ragged drunks swilling beer from tin pails, and dirty toddlers playing in greasy, littered stairwells.

The look of *Regeneration* recalls both the photographs of social reformer Jacob Riis, whose *How the Other Half Lives* (1890) shocked viewers by exposing the abject poverty in New York's slums, and the paintings of the Ashcan School. Around the turn of the twentieth century, artists like George Bellows and George Luks painted street scenes, tenements, boxing clubs, saloons, docks, and construction sites, celebrating the vigor and vitality of working-class urban life, a style Walsh echoed with red-blooded brio. Working with French cinematographer Georges Benoît, he captured marvelous

Raoul Walsh's *Regeneration* captured the menace of New York's Lower East Side slums with gritty flair, recalling Jacob Riis's iconic 1888 photograph "Bandits' Roost, 59 ½ Mulberry Street" (page 60), an image that Martin Scorsese later reproduced in *Gangs of New York* (2002).

scenes of swarming streets, kids playing on fire escapes, docks jostling with cranes and tugboats. An excursion-boat disaster based on the 1904 sinking of the General Slocum is staged with alarming verisimilitude, with extras leaping off the ship to escape raging flames—though the sequence is given an ahistorical happy ending ("All the kiddies were saved").

Against this backdrop of raw realism, the central story of moral reformation feels even more creakily Victorian, especially the flawless nobility and purity of Marie (i.e., "Mamie Rose"), played by the angelically beautiful Anna Q. Nilsson. The stage actor Rockliffe Fellowes is charismatic as Owen, even if he seems a little too affable and clean-cut to be leading a gang of thugs. The villain, Skinny (William Sheer), is a far more persuasive lowlife, with his gaunt face, ratlike teeth, and eye patch (eerily prefiguring the one Walsh would wear after losing an eye in 1928). The plot change that so upset Kildare greatly strengthens the story: Owen's dilemma when Skinny pleads for protection after knifing a cop pits old debts and deep-rooted loyalties against his desire to keep Marie's respect. His choice has dire consequences, leading to a fatal showdown between the two men when Skinny assaults Marie.

Raoul Walsh gave up acting after he lost his right eye in 1928, thanks to a jackrabbit that hit the windshield of his car while he was driving in Arizona.

Walsh's mastery of action is displayed in a magnificent long shot capturing Skinny's attempt to escape via one of the dozens of clotheslines stretched between two cliff-like tenements. But nothing prepares you for the shock close-up after he falls: his face a gruesome death mask with blood running from the mouth, one eye wide open and the other a hollow socket. Movies would wrestle for decades with how graphic they should be, and while they have ultimately come down on the side of explicitness, the question remains: how much realism do audiences want, and how much truth can they handle?

No Escape: *I Am a Fugitive from a Chain Gang* (1932) and 1930s Social Realism

Prohibition, which took effect in 1920, had many unintended consequences: it spawned an enormous rise in organized crime and gangland violence, and the nation's fascination with the underworld in turn boosted the genre of true crime. In 1924, editor Bernarr Macfadden founded the pioneering *True Detective Mysteries*, initially publishing a mix of fiction and nonfiction stories. Around 1930, he phased out the fiction to focus solely on true crime. Accounts of Prohibition-era violence, and the pulp stories and hardboiled novels inspired by them—like the two classic books James M. Cain spun out of Ruth Snyder's 1927 plot to murder her husband—would provide fodder for many postwar noir films.

In 1931, *True Detective Mysteries* serialized a sensational first-person story by Robert Elliott Burns, which was published in book form in 1932 as *I Am a Fugitive from a Chain Gang!* and turned into a film the same year at Warner Bros., directed by Mervyn LeRoy. Burns, who was sentenced to ten years' hard labor for a petty stickup that he insisted he had been tricked into by an acquaintance,

In 1932, Paul Muni was Oscar-nominated for his performance as James Allen, and the same year played the brutal gangster Tony Camonte in Howard Hawks's *Scarface*.

According to his brother, Robert E. Burns suffered from what we would now term PTSD after his service in World War I, leading him to become a drifter.

exposed the hellish conditions in southern prison camps, from which he had twice escaped. LeRoy's film, lensed by Sol Polito and anchored by Paul Muni's searing performance, has a rough, drab, documentary look, and wisely makes no attempt to inject any lightness or humor into the story. Although the film spans the end of World War I to the present, the whole affair is suffused with a Depression-era mood of desperation and hopelessness. Muni's character, renamed James Allen, seems trapped from the get-go, when he flees a soul-crushing factory job to become a drifter. The single mistake that dooms him is trying to run when the cops burst in during the stickup; because of it, he must keep running forever.

Committed to authenticity, Muni met with Burns, who served as a consultant on the film, and studied the way he walked and talked, aiming to capture the "smell of fear" that clung to him. (Burns was still wanted in Georgia, but the film's success emboldened him to make public appearances denouncing the chain-gang system.) Muni also did intensive research into the southern penal system, meeting with guards who had worked at camps like the ones depicted. He gives his most naturalistic performance, matching the film's verité style, which relies on archival stock footage to give the feeling of a newsreel. As Allen wanders the country, he encounters nothing but trains, construction sites, flophouses, lunch wagons, and pawn shops overflowing with medals hocked by veterans.

Once he gets to the prison camp, the movie takes its time letting us absorb the full horror. We observe how the convicts' shackles are hammered on and checked each day, and the awkward way the chains force them to hobble. We see how the work gangs are loaded onto trucks in the predawn darkness; and how long "bull chains" are run through rings on the men's shackles, pulled through with a chilling sound like a metallic death rattle. We see the convicts spread out across the glaring sweep of a quarry, breaking rocks in the heat and dust. In a period when most Hollywood films were still studio-bound, these scenes display the kind of unvarnished candor seen in photographs of Dustbowl migrants taken for the Farm Security Administration by artists such as Dorothea Lange and Margaret Bourke-White. During Allen's first escape, suspense is heightened by the lack of music, natural set-

Chicago-born Muni got his start in Yiddish Theatre as Muni Weisenfreund. An uncredited Everett Brown played Sebastian, the Black inmate who helps Allen escape.

ting, and stripped-down urgency: there is only the sound of dogs baying and blurry traveling shots as he pelts through dusty, sun-splashed underbrush.

His liberty is short-lived, since he is blackmailed into marriage by a gold-digging woman who threatens to turn him in if he leaves her. Having become a successful engineer, he tells another woman that he wants to build roads and bridges so that people can get away. (In reality, after his first escape Burns became a newspaper editor.) When Allen is tricked into returning voluntarily to captivity—assured he will get a pardon if he serves sixty days, only to find that Georgia intends to make him serve out his full ten years of hard labor as revenge for his exposure of the system—he manages to escape again. His disillusionment is symbolized by his blowing up a bridge during his getaway, destroying what he had hoped to build.

I Am a Fugitive from a Chain Gang was not only a critical success, praised for its "stark realism" and "unflinching realism," and nominated for a bouquet of awards; it was also a big moneymaker for Warner Bros., proving wrong Roy Del Ruth, who had turned down an offer to direct the film on the grounds that it was the wrong time to make such a depressing movie, that audiences craved escape. The only people who did not like the film were prison authorities in Georgia, who protested that they had been unfairly maligned. Yet the movie does not even touch on the most shameful aspect of the "convict leasing" system: the fact that it was a source of revenue for the state, a legal form of slavery. As Allen cries out after being returned to the chain gang, "Their crimes are worse than anyone here."

Made at a time when the case was still unresolved, *I Am a Fugitive from a Chain Gang* is a rare example of a movie based on a true story whose ending is more downbeat than what really happened. Burns was arrested again in 1932, but the governor of New Jersey (Burns's home state, where he had returned) refused to extradite him; thanks to the book and the movie, public opinion was solidly on his side. The fugitive married again and started a family, finally obtaining a commutation of his sentence to time served in 1943, with the help of the newly elected Georgia governor Ellis Arnall. He lived out the rest of his life a free man.

The film forgoes any optimism, distilling all the pessimism and disillusionment of 1932—the worst year of the Depression—into one of the most powerful endings in cinema. After a montage of newspaper headlines speculating on the whereabouts of the fugitive, Allen materializes out of the night to speak with Helen (Helen Vinson), the woman he loves. In an anguished, ripped-from-the-guts speech, he tells her that even though he escaped, "They're still after me. They'll always be after me. I hide in rooms all day and travel by night. No friends, no rest, no peace. Keep moving, that's all that's left for me." She begs him to stay, but he retreats into the shadows, dissolving into the darkness as he slips away. "How do you live?" she asks, and his answer—"I steal!"—comes from a black void.

It is not always factual accuracy or documentary plainness that add up to truth: it takes art to make a moment so piercingly true to a whole nation's sense of loss, shame, and fear.

Just the Facts: *Call Northside 777* (1948) and Postwar Semi-documentaries

I Am a Fugitive from a Chain Gang could never have been made after 1934, when the Motion Picture Production Code began to be strictly enforced. While the Code only dealt with the content of movies, Hollywood films began to look different too: more polished, more classical, with all the rough edges sanded off. By the mid-1940s, after a decade of glossy and airless studio perfection, seeing real, ordinary places on-screen was cause for excitement. One of the most enthusiastic champions of the postwar movement to bring documentary elements into movies was writer James Agee, who lavishly praised Elia Kazan's *Boomerang!* (1947), one of the earliest examples of the trend. That same year, he wrote, "One of the best things that is happening in Hollywood is the tendency to move out of the place—to base fictional pictures on fact, and, more importantly, to shoot them not in painted studio sets but in actual places."

The public's appetite for realism had been whetted by the great combat documentaries made during World War II, while many filmmakers were inspired by the radical, emotionally shattering works of Italian neorealism (such as Vittorio De Sica's *Shoeshine* [1946] and *Bicycle Thieves* [1948]), which used nonprofessional actors and location shooting to tell stories stripped of any comforting illusions. Framing crime dramas with stentorian narrators boasting of films' adherence to facts, or prologues featuring sclerotic civil servants speechifying in their offices was also a way to appease the Production Code's requirement that movies uphold law, order, and virtue. It evidently didn't occur to the censors that audiences merely sat through these sermons in order to get to the good parts—gangsters, violence, seedy settings, and inky shadows.

The "semi-documentary" style ("pseudo-documentary" might be more accurate) took firm root at 20th Century-Fox, thanks largely to producer Louis de Rochemont, the creator of the *March of Time* newsreel series. De Rochemont produced *Boomerang!*, and the studio followed up the next year with Henry Hathaway's *Call Northside 777*; both films were based on real cases of men wrongfully accused of crimes, and were shot on location, sometimes in the actual spots where the events had taken place. (See Eddie Muller's survey *Ripped From the Headlines!* beginning on page 78 for a discussion of Kazan's film.) Focusing on innocent men whose names are eventually cleared was a way to make crime movies under the Production Code that could have happy endings; but exposing the failures and callousness of the justice system directly challenged the Code's emphasis on showing respect for authorities and institutions. Insisting on these stories' factual basis only made the challenge bolder.

Call Northside 777 changed names but hewed fairly close to the facts in its account of a case that started in 1932 with the fatal shooting of a Chicago policeman in a speakeasy, part of the cresting wave of violent crime that finally led to the repeal of Prohibition one year later. Two men, Joseph Majczek and Theodore Marcinkiewicz, were convicted of the killing and had served eleven years in jail when, in 1944, two *Chicago Times* reporters spotted an ad placed by Majczek's mother, Tillie, offering $5,000

for information on the killing. Smelling human interest in the story of a devoted mother who had saved the money by working as a scrubwoman, they delved into the case, their investigation ultimately leading to the men's release—though not to the identity of the real killer, who was never found. In the film, the reporter played by James Stewart starts out cynically dismissive, only gradually convinced that a gross injustice has been done as he discovers the men were railroaded on the dubious testimony of a single witness, the bitter and defiantly spiteful Wanda Skutnik (Betty Garde).

Joseph MacDonald's crisp cinematography makes excellent use of Chicago locations far afield from icons like the Wrigley Building. Stewart's legwork takes him through the city's Polish neighborhoods, with their shabby wood-frame houses and ornate Catholic churches, and on a crawl through the dive bars behind the stockyards, where you can smell the stale beer and sweat. He also experiences the oppressive sterility and surveillance of the panopticon in Joliet's Stateville Prison. The film has a newspaper's blend of diligent fact-gathering punched up with local color, boldface urgency, and op-ed pleading. Its documentary aesthetic is wedded to an enthusiastic faith in the promise of technology to uncover truth, which feels sadly antiquated today. The crucial piece of evidence that turns the tide comes from a journalistic photograph that is enlarged until the date on a newspaper can be read. (This twist was invented for the movie.) In another scene, Leonarde Keeler, the inventor of the polygraph, appears as himself, administering a lie-detector test to Frank Wiecek (Richard Conte, playing the character based on Majczek). The reliability of polygraph tests has since been called into question, but Conte gives the scene an intense, visceral charge as Wiecek tries to control his own breathing and pulse in order to prove his honesty.

You can't always judge whether movies are telling the truth from the way they look. Some films that veer far afield from realism have roots in factual cases, like the southern gothic fairy tale *The Night of the Hunter* (1955). Plenty of noir films used location shooting and documentary techniques to tell entirely fictional stories, like Jules Dassin's *The Naked City* (1948). Producer Mark Hellinger purchased the rights to the freelance press photographer Arthur Fellig's 1945 photobook just so that he could use the title, but Dassin recreated certain trademark images by the era's greatest snatcher of crime-scene pictures and poet laureate of urban gawking, who styled himself Weegee the Famous.

Today, when photos and videos can be made to lie, and movies increasingly rely on images animated by a computer rather than recorded by a camera, the distinction between fact and fantasy, reality and make-believe, keeps getting murkier. Many people seem not to care. That's the true crime. ■

Call Northside 777 was James Stewart's first venture into film noir, while Richard Conte was a mainstay of crime dramas throughout the 1940s and '50s.

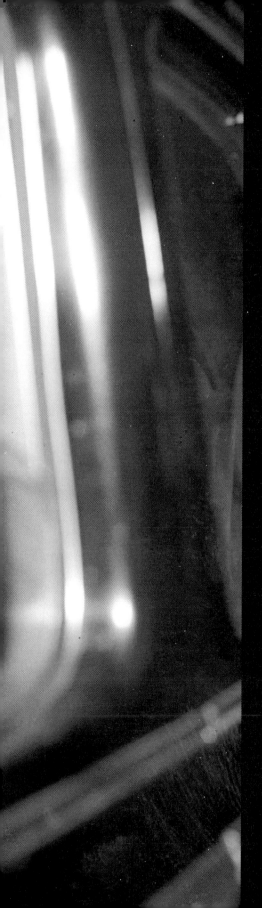

BURY THE PAST

Land Swindles. Chicago Mobsters. A Prison Break. A Suppressed Movie. And America's Cosmetics Kingpin? Take a wild ride through the tumultuous story of *Roger Touhy, Gangster*.

By John Wranovics

Maksymilian Faktorowicz, born in Poland in the 1870s, found initial success in Moscow, as a wigmaker. Later, after he'd moved to Los Angeles and changed his name to Max Factor, he claimed to have been the cosmetician for the czar of Russia's extended family, as well as the Imperial Russian Grand Opera. Attracted to the nascent Hollywood film industry, Max Factor established himself as a preeminent maker of theatrical cosmetics and wigs. He developed a new ultra-thin facial cream—ideal for film performers—which quickly replaced the thick, pasty make-up commonly used (and notorious for cracking). As color film emerged in the late 1920s, the new emulsion often cast a reddish tint on actors' made-up faces.

Factor solved this by developing a new product called Pan-Cake. By the time he died in 1938, a demise hastened by a car accident two years earlier, Max Factor was known across America as the King of Cosmetics.

Impressive. But it's Max Factor's younger half-brother, Iakov Faktorowicz, who holds more interest for this publication. His birthplace is uncertain—either England or Poland, probably sometime in late 1892. At the age of fourteen, Iakov would change his name to John Factor after emigrating with his family to the United States and settling in St. Louis.

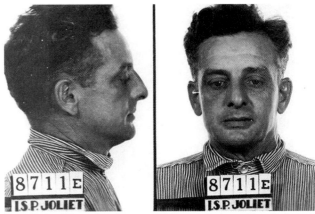

Roger Touhy, Chicago beer baron and Al Capone rival, spent twenty-five years in prison for the alleged kidnapping of John Factor.

A born entrepreneur, John Factor started his career benignly, working as a newsboy, bootblack, and livery stable water boy. But his fortunes changed in 1916 when he moved to Chicago and opened a three-chair barber shop in Halsted Street on Chicago's West Side, charging only five cents for a haircut and a dime for a shave. By the late 1920s, he was simply known as "Jake the Barber." He used the shop's profits to promote oil land deals in the Southwest. A 1928 news item referred to him as "the notorious share pusher and arch swindler." Fellow crooks called him the "Master Crook of the Decade." John Factor soon moved into Florida real estate, selling $5 million worth of "ocean land." Indictments followed as $1 million worth of that land was underwater.

To flee the heat, Jake the Barber secured the aid of New York racketeer Jack "Legs" Diamond, who grubstaked his escape to Europe. Apparently, the gangster and the "smooth-talking ex-barber" had an agreement under which Diamond financed Factor's swindles in exchange for a split of the profits. By some estimates, Factor pilfered anywhere from $5–12 million. But his big mistake was snubbing Diamond.

In 1931, the Associated Press reported that Diamond had put a price on Factor's head, and that the Barber "might be slain before he could be arrested for extradition to England, where he is accused of defrauding investors of several millions of dollars." Making Diamond even angrier was that during his trip to Europe to search for the elusive Factor, he was shot five times. Newspapers reported that "greedy gangsters . . . having heard that Factor had made $12,000,000, were seeking to kidnap him for ransom." News items declared that "gangs in New York, St. Louis, and Chicago had been hunting Factor for weeks to kidnap him, knowing he made millions in Europe and could pay huge ransoms—yet could not appeal to police for protection because the police wanted him also."

Factor eventually snuck back into Chicago and solicited protection from Al Capone. Meanwhile, he was tried in absentia in England and sentenced to twenty-four years in prison. Jake the Barber would fight his extradition all the way up until 1962, when President John F. Kennedy issued him a full pardon. It was later revealed that Factor was the single largest contributor to Kennedy's election campaign.

FLASHBACK: On April 18, 1933, Jake the Barber's son, Jerome, was kidnapped—the same day the US Supreme Court was hearing arguments about the Barber's extradition. Some believe the kidnapping had been faked in an attempt to stall the court's decision. If so, the ploy worked—the Supreme Court held the case over for reargument at a later date.

Perhaps inspired by the results of young Jerome's "kidnapping," Factor himself was reputedly kidnapped on June 30, 1933—at least, he disappeared for several weeks. Blame for the alleged crime was

After the FBI's Melvin Purvis failed to pin the Hamm kidnapping on Touhy (far right) and cronies, Touhy was the perfect fallguy for the John Factor snatch.

placed on a Cicero-based beer baron and Capone rival named Roger "the Terrible" Touhy, described in a 1933 newspaper exposé as "public enemy, alcohol czar, and roadhouse overlord."

On December 4, 1933, the Supreme Court ordered that John Factor be remanded to British authorities to face charges for fraudulent land swindles. He was taken into custody on April 17, 1934. But US Secretary of State Cordell Hull, encouraged by the Chicago police, arranged for Factor's release—so he could testify as a witness against Roger Touhy. A month prior, Touhy and some cronies had beaten the rap for the kidnapping of William A. Hamm, Jr., millionaire president of the Hamm Brewing Company. But on February 23, 1934, Touhy, Basil "The Owl" Banghart, and two others were convicted for Jake's alleged kidnapping. Touhy and Banghart were sentenced to ninety-nine years at Stateville Prison in Joliet. For the rest of his life, Touhy argued that the kidnapping was a frame job orchestrated by his rival, Capone.

After three months on the lam, the FBI caught up with Touhy, killing two of his fellow prison escapees in the raid.

On October 9, 1942, the country was galvanized by news reports of Roger Touhy's escape from Stateville. Along with Banghart and five others, Touhy had busted out with a few smuggled guns and a tall ladder. Within a week, according to the FBI, "[J. Edgar Hoover] directed a continent-wide man hunt that had no equal since the days of Dillinger." Touhy and his fellow escapees, however, were *state* prisoners—their escape violated no *federal* law. But the FBI was able to circumvent the jurisdictional

Roger Touhy, Gangster: The Movie

Just 65 minutes long, *Roger Touhy, Gangster* (1944) begins like . . . well, like gangbusters. After scrolling text absolves the FBI of any blame or credit for what's to follow—and thanks the governor of Illinois and the Joliet prison's warden for their support in the film's making—the screen erupts in a 45-second montage of machine-gun bullets, bombs, and screeching black sedans. The images recall the prewar heyday of gangster films, many made at Warner Bros., where Bryan Foy ran the B unit in the 1930s. Now at 20th Century-Fox, Foy intended *Roger Touhy, Gangster* to deliver a new level of realism to crime pictures. As one critic wrote, the film was "a new type of gangster picture, an unadorned film biography of a public enemy." James Agee noted, however, that "*Touhy* has some fairly exciting and intelligent things in it, and anyone who loves the best of the old gangster films will get some nostalgic pleasure out of it; but it is a long way short even of the ordinary ones in immediacy, drive, tension, and imagination."

Foy had planned to cast Lloyd Nolan, Anthony Quinn, Preston Foster, and Reed Hadley, all from the roster of his last picture, *Guadalcanal Diary* (1943). But Nolan balked and Foster, who'd played a humble and heroic priest in *Guadalcanal Diary*, ended up with the lead role. He portrays Touhy as uneducated, violent, superstitious, and humorless. If it was Foy's purpose, in support of his own Chicago mob cronies, to drain any redeeming qualities from the gangster's reputation, the film is an unqualified success. The only levity comes from character actor Frank "Off-the-Cuff" Jenks, who plays Touhy gang member "Troubles" O'Connor. Cy Kendall brings a strange edginess to his uncredited role as the partner of Touhy's kidnap victim, Joe Sutton, who is played with no energy and little imagination by William Post Jr. By contrast, Group Theatre veteran Henry Morgan, in the cheap-creep mode common in some of his earliest roles, delivers the goods as the gang's traitor, "Smoke" Reardon, who helps send his fellow "Touhy Terribles" up the river. Eight years after testifying against Touhy, Smoke finds himself in Stateville Prison with the rest of the gang ("I guess you guys are pretty sore"). When the terrified stool pigeon gets killed (offscreen, surprisingly), Touhy loses his last best chance of having his conviction overturned—and so the prison break is put in motion.

As Touhy's right-hand man "The Owl" Banghart, Victor McLaglen is hard to buy as a former teacher obsessed with correcting everyone's grammar. One critic described it as "an inverse comedy technique of speaking Oxonian English through his battered nose." Director Robert Florey had made experimental films in the 1920s, some with famed master of montage, Slavko Vorkapich. Here, he goes montage-mad from the start, filling what seems like a third of the film with quick-cut edits to display the end of Prohibition and the daily life of the prison population. Much is made out of the location shots of the actual prison—a novelty at the time—but frequent use of rear projection proves distracting and awkward.

For its time, *Roger Touhy, Gangster* was noteworthy for trying to deromanticize the gangster hero and bring more realism to the genre. One critic wrote, "The picture is presented in straightforward reportorial style, which gives the authority of a documentary film." But, like the "hangdog surrender" the fugitives make to the feds at the film's end, the movie deflates—giving in to moralizing speeches from Stateville's actual warden about the wages of sin. For this one, Bryan Foy, famed King of Bs, deserves a *B* grade, at best.

—*John Wranovics*

issue since the fugitives failed to present themselves for registration under the Selective Service law, and draft dodging was a federal offense. The gang was soon captured by G-men in Chicago, with two of the escapees dying in the shootout. Banghart, confronted by Hoover, told the FBI director: "You're much fatter than you are on the radio." Touhy was returned to Stateville with 100 more years tacked on to his original 99 year sentence.

The Movie Version

By late 1942, mob-friendly producer Bryan Foy, now at 20th Century-Fox after years heading the B unit at Warner Bros., was developing *Prison Break*, the latest in a series of prison pictures made in collaboration with writer Crane Wilbur. Foy, a close friend of Capone operatives Johnny Roselli and Allen Smiley, immediately recognized the "ripped from the headlines" angle that Roger Touhy's bust-out presented, and the pair reshaped the project as *The Life of Touhy*. Lloyd Nolan, Victor McLaglen, Preston Foster, and Anthony Quinn were announced as stars—until a March 17, 1943, *Hollywood Reporter* item announced that Nolan, cast as Roger Touhy, was withdrawing to take "a stand against portraying any more screen gunmen." That May, studio PR noted that Quinn would play the informer Smoke Reardon, a role that ended up going to Henry Morgan. Quinn was cast instead as George Carroll, Touhy's Stateville cellmate. The switch happened when "it was called to Producer [Lee] Marcus' attention that Quinn is one of the very few Latin-American actors of any prominence in Hollywood and it would not be conducive to inter-American amity to have him as such a despicable character."

For a while it appeared that Kent Taylor, a screen veteran, would get the title role in what was now being called *Roger Touhy, Last of the Gangsters*. Unfortunately for Taylor, he had to trade roles with Foster, since the close-cropped haircut Taylor had adopted for his previous role as a Nazi agent hadn't grown out.

Original director Eugene Forde was replaced by Robert Florey, who'd previously worked for Foy on *Dangerously They Live* (1941) and *Lady Gangster* (1942). Florey and Foy were given unprecedented access to Stateville Prison. "Foy and Director Robert Florey not only got to photograph the state penitentiary and many of its 5,000 inmates," noted a news item, "but even the prison garbage truck and the ladder used by the Touhy gang in their sensational jail break last October." Florey later noted that the film's shooting schedule ran an extra two weeks "on account of all the searching. One day I was searched sixteen times. It took me two hours once to get permission to walk through one door. And many of the prisoners refused to show their faces to the camera. It was a very depressing experience."

Touhy went to court to fight against the film's release. On August 4, 1943, he won an injunction preventing 20th Century-Fox from advertising or exhibiting the movie. A couple of days later, the

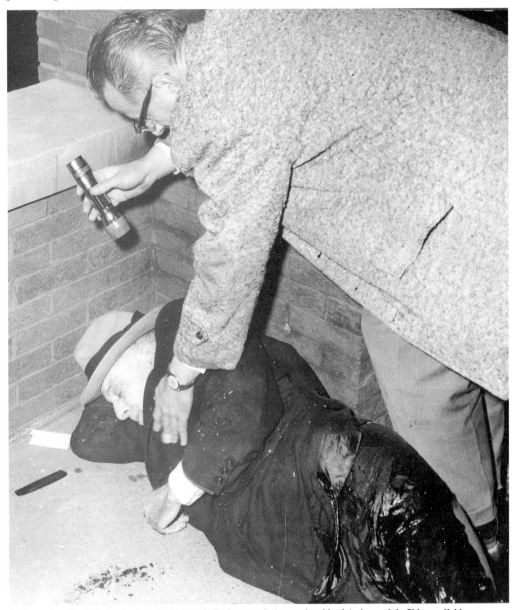

On December 16, 1959, free for less than a month, Touhy was shotgunned on his sister's porch in Chicago. He'd contended that the Factor kidnapping was a hoax until the very end.

injunction was lifted on the grounds that Touhy "had not contended that the film portrayed him falsely." Touhy filed an amended injunction, which was quickly rejected by the court.

The FBI also stalled the film's release, protesting that the movie gave undue credit to local law enforcement when the plaudits properly belonged to the bureau. The FBI demanded that the studio reshoot parts of the film. An article in February 1944 reported, "*Roger Touhy, Gangster* . . . made nearly a year ago, is still . . . on the shelf at 20th Century-Fox. Not only does Touhy, in prison at Joliet, Ill., threaten an injunction preventing its showing, but the FBI has objected to the way its agents acted in the run-down. Bryan Foy, producer, just returned from an FBI conference in Washington, plans to shoot some added scenes."

The completed film had its premiere at Stateville Prison on July 12, 1944. Touhy refused to watch it, opting to remain in his cell. Also skipping the show was John "Jake the Barber" Factor, renamed Joe Sutton in the movie. Factor had just begun a ten-year sentence for mail fraud, having been convicted of reselling bonded whiskey certificates. The premiere (which included over a thousand invited guests) suffered setbacks when Touhy's compatriots cut the power supply to the speakers and radiator valves were pried opened to feed steam into the sweltering auditorium. Showtime was delayed by almost 90 minutes.

The film received positive reviews when it appeared in theaters that summer. But Touhy's family was ultimately successful in stanching its circulation, settling a lawsuit for defamation against Fox and Chicago's Balaban and Katz Theater Corporation, suing each for $500,000. Touhy settled for $15,000 and the understanding that 20th Century-Fox would destroy the film and never distribute it again in the United States.

In 1954, Touhy succeeded in getting US district judge John P. Barnes to rule that John Factor had faked his own kidnapping. Barnes's decision was overruled by an appeals court, but in 1959, after serving more than twenty-five years for a kidnapping he always maintained had been a set-up, Touhy—now sixty-one—was released from Stateville. Twenty-three days later, on December 16, 1959, he was shotgunned to death on the porch of his sister's home.

Jake the Barber was released from prison in 1949. By 1955, he and his wife, Rella, were in charge of the Stardust Hotel in Las Vegas, which was secretly controlled by Chicago mob bosses Paul Ricca, Tony Accardo, Murray Humphreys, and Sam Giancana. Foy's good buddy Johnny Roselli would later tell LA-based mobster Jimmy Fratianno, "I got the Stardust for Chicago." During Factor's tenure at the hotel-casino, from 1955–63, the Justice Department estimated that the Chicago outfit skimmed between $48–200 million dollars from the Stardust alone.

By the mid-1970s, *Roger Touhy, Gangster* was starting to regularly appear on television; Touhy's estate sued CBS, Fox, and Balaban and Katz for breach of contract. The estate alleged that under the provisions of the settlement reached in 1949, "Twentieth Century-Fox had agreed that the film was never to be shown within the U.S. but was to be destroyed." In 1979, the court ruled against the Touhy estate.

John Factor's final years were spent rehabilitating his reputation as a "noted philanthropist" who spent his fortune on a wide range of charities. When he died in 1984, at age ninety-one, four hundred people attended his funeral. California governor Edmund G. "Pat" Brown and Los Angeles mayor Tom Bradley gave eulogies.

In the early 1960s, confronted by a *Los Angeles Times* reporter probing his criminal history, Jake the Barber had wept, asking, "How much does a man have to do to bury his past?" His remains now reside in the Hollywood Forever Cemetery. ∎

RIPPED FROM THE HEADLINES!

Starting in 1934, strict enforcement of the Motion Picture Production Code mandated that moviemakers steer clear of stories based on actual crimes. Concern over "glorification" of criminal behavior began to dissipate, however, during the film noir movement. **EDDIE MULLER** offers a selective survey of significant fact-based noirs that paved the way for today's abundance of true crime tales.

Dillinger (1945)

Hollywood's bosses made a pact in 1935 to not produce films about actual outlaws—especially John Dillinger, whose Robin Hood persona captured the public's imagination during the Depression. The King Brothers thumbed their noses at that edict ten years later with this down-and-dirty depiction of Dillinger's exploits. Phil Yordan's Oscar-nominated script took a just-the-facts approach, eschewing moralizing. Though the film was mostly cobbled together from stock footage (one robbery is lifted from 1937's *You Only Live Once*), Lawrence Tierney's malevolent performance as Public Enemy #1 made *Dillinger* a smash. Veteran director Frank Borzage, however, excoriated the film and public guardians demanded the prints be destroyed. The Kings laughed all the way to the bank—yet it would be more than a decade before Dillinger reappeared on-screen, played by Leo Gordon in 1957's *Baby Face Nelson* (with Mickey Rooney in the title role), part of a pent-up wave of late 1950s gangster bios that included *The Scarface Mob* (1959), *Al Capone* (1959), *The Rise and Fall of Legs Diamond* (1960), and *Murder, Inc.* (1960).

Boomerang! (1947)

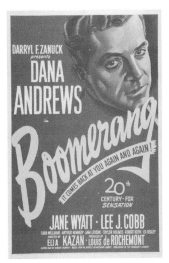

The safer strategy for true crime adaptations in postwar Hollywood was to focus on do-gooders righting miscarriages of justice. 20th Century-Fox chief Darryl Zanuck, with producer Louis de Rochemont, pioneered the "semi-documentary" approach to crime with *The House on 92nd Street* (1945), conjoining actual FBI cases of home-front espionage. *Boomerang!*, made two years later, was based on the 1924 case of Harold Israel, a vagrant accused of murdering Catholic priest Hubert Dahme in Bridgeport, Connecticut. Richard Murphy's Oscar-nominated screenplay described the political pressure brought on skeptical prosecutor Henry Harvey (Dana Andrews), who was expected to win a fast conviction. Opposition in Bridgeport to the story's retelling forced location shooting to nearby Stamford. The film is notable for *not* solving the crime—the DA ends up intentionally exonerating the suspect he's supposed to convict. The actual case remains unsolved. The real-life prosecutor, Homer Cummings, gained sufficient notoriety to become a player in Democratic party politics and in 1933 was appointed attorney general by President Roosevelt. 20th Century-Fox followed the success of *Boomerang!* with *Call Northside 777* (1948), another semi-documentary retelling of a real-life crime (learn more about that case and film in Imogen Sara Smith's article, page 60).

Canon City (1948)

The breakout of twelve convicts from the federal prison in Canon (pronounced "canyon") City, Colorado, on December 30, 1947, gave writer-director Crane Wilbur inspiration for yet another prison yarn. Wilbur, "the Potentate of Prison Pictures," had been writing men-behind-bars sagas since the 1930s. What made this one historically significant is that it was done in partnership with Eagle-

Lion producer Bryan Foy and "silent partner" Johnny Roselli, the Chicago mob's man in Hollywood. It starts as a faux documentary (Warden Roy Best playing himself) but soon becomes full-on noir—photographed by John Alton—with vignettes tracking the desperate fugitives. Poster art promised explosive violence, but the film is a hushed and sweaty affair. It kills a few cons for dramatic effect, but in actuality the escapees were all recaptured within the week. *LIFE* later ran a photo of them back in stir, watching *Canon City* on movie night. Jim Sherbondy, the reluctant escapee played by Scott Brady, remained in the state's penal system until 1969, when he was killed trying to escape from a prison work farm.

He Walked by Night (1948)

Bryan Foy, Crane Wilbur, and Johnny Roselli strike again. Wilbur developed the film from the real-life story of Erwin Walker, a war vet and police dispatcher who was a one-man crime wave in postwar Los Angeles, PTSD psychosis leading him on a yearlong spree stealing weapons and electronics. It culminated in his killing highway patrolman Loren Roosevelt on June 5, 1946. In custody, Walker claimed he was inventing a ray gun that turned metal to dust, making it too costly to fight more wars. More interesting to Wilbur were the forensics of the manhunt and how Walker had used sewers to evade capture. Famously Jack Webb, who played a police lab technician, used the film as inspiration for his *Dragnet* radio and television shows. Walker was judged sane and sentenced to the gas chamber. Days before execution, Walker tried to hang himself; a psychiatrist declared him a "paranoid schizophrenic." Doctors worked to return his sanity—so the state could execute him. Instead, Walker became a model prisoner, and was paroled in 1974. He changed his name, worked as a chemist, and lived to be ninety-one.

The Undercover Man (1949)

While the FBI forbade films being made about Al Capone, Columbia circumvented that with *The Undercover Man*. It was based on Frank Wilson, the Treasury agent who brought down Capone for income tax evasion. Elmer Irey, who led the investigative team during Capone's prosecution, said that Wilson "fears nothing that walks. He will sit quietly looking at books eighteen hours a day, seven days a week—forever, if he wants to find something in those books." Not even as kinetic a director as Joseph H. Lewis, nor an actor as charismatic as Glenn Ford, could put much life into such a by-the-book hero.

Richard Basehart gives a tour-de-force performance as Roy Martin, a psychotic loner based on the real-life Erwin Walker, whose actual story was far more complex than the movie based on his notorious Los Angeles crime spree. Scott Brady is the KO victim in this scene.

Capone, renamed Salvatore Rocco (Anthony Caruso), is relegated to a supporting role, the story's focus sticking with the paper-chasing feds. It would be another ten years before Hollywood tried to tackle Capone's saga. Nicholas Ray's *Party Girl* (1958) had Lee J. Cobb's Rico Angelo as a Capone surrogate. *The Scarface Mob* (1959) pitted Eliot Ness (Robert Stack) against Capone (Neville Brand), and Rod Steiger chewed all available scenery as *Al Capone* (1959), which told the tale from his POV—a no-no ten years earlier.

Lonely Heart Bandits (1950)

This obscure Republic B is a historical footnote for being the first film based on the notorious exploits of serial killers Ray Fernandez and Martha Beck. Between 1947 and 1949, the pair, pretending to be brother and sister, preyed on women who placed "lonely heart" ads in newspapers. They were arrested March 1, 1949, and although suspected of as many as seventeen murders, were tried only for the murder of sixty-six-year-old Janet Fay. Fernandez and Beck were executed in Sing Sing on March 8, 1951, six months after the release of *Lonely Heart Bandits*. The 60-minute B, directed by George Blair and starring John Eldredge and Dorothy Patrick as the renamed killer-lovers, is a sanitized version of the gruesome reality, which never could have been depicted in the Code-dominated era. Once the PCA was dead, however, the tale was resurrected many times: *The Honeymoon Killers* (1970), *Deep Crimson* (Mexico, 1996), *Lonely Hearts* (2006), and *Alleluia* (Belgium, 2014) are all imaginative and bloody interpretations of the story.

Highway 301 (1950)

By 1950, Bryan Foy was back at Warner Bros., where in the 1930s he ran the studio's B unit. He found another true crime aficionado in writer-director Andrew Stone, who'd knocked around Hollywood since the silent era. Stone anticipated the rise of independent films and knew crime stories offered good return on investment in a system starting to crack apart. He pitched Foy a yarn from a file of 1,500 true crime cases he'd collected. The result was a brutal depiction of the Tri-State Gang, who in 1934 robbed and killed their way through Pennsylvania, Maryland, and Virginia. Leader Walter Legenza (Steve Cochran) briefly nudged Dillinger from the top of the FBI's "Most Wanted" list. The film takes viewers hostage on a crime spree that turns shockingly violent. The real Legenza was arrested in 1934, convicted, and sentenced to death. Weeks before execution, he had guns smuggled into the jail in a canned chicken. He and cohort Robert Mais shot their way out, rampaging for another three months. Once recaptured, they were electrocuted within the week.

Try and Get Me! (1951)

In 1933, Harold Thurmond and Jack Holmes kidnapped Brooke Hart, scion of a San Jose mercantile family. They demanded $40,000 for his return—although Hart had already been drowned. Captured, Thurmond and Holmes blamed each other for Hart's "accident," leading the press to speculate on a possible mistrial or an acquittal for one of the men. Riled up by the speculation, citizens descended on the jail. The sheriff begged Governor James Rolph to have the National Guard keep the peace. Rolph refused. The mob overran the cops, dragged Thurmond and Holmes from their cells, and hanged them in the town square. Rolph praised the mob for saving taxpayers the trouble. Producer Robert Stillman bought *The Condemned*, Jo Pagano's 1947 novel about the incident, because of parallels between mob lynching and current anti-Communist hysteria. Director Cy Endfield, soon blacklisted himself, kept an intense focus on the Thurmond character, renamed Howard Tyler (Frank Lovejoy), making this tale of a desperate man's spiral into hell perhaps the bleakest noir ever.

Fourteen Hours (1951)

On July 26, 1938, John Warde brought downtown Manhattan to a standstill as he perched on the seventeenth-floor ledge of the Gotham Hotel threatening to jump. The first officer at the scene, Charles Glasco, consoled the young man for fourteen hours, but couldn't save him; Warde leapt (or fell) to his death. In the film version (written by John Paxton, directed by Henry Hathaway), suicidal Robert Cosick (Richard Basehart) teeters on the ledge as a callous city gawks. Despite the efforts of Officer Dunnigan (Paul Douglas) to talk him down, Cosick falls to his death. In the last shot, a sanitation truck washes away his splattered remains. At least that's what audiences saw at the film's premiere. That same day in New York, the daughter of 20th Century-Fox president Spyros Skouras killed herself by leaping from her room in Bellevue Hospital. Devastated, Skouras ordered *Fourteen Hours* pulled from theaters. Darryl Zanuck saved the studio's investment, rounding up a few actors and a skeleton crew (Basehart not among them) and shooting a new ending in which Cosick is whisked to safety.

I Was a Communist for the FBI (1951)

The Communist witch hunt required at least one "true crime" exposé. Again, Foy and Wilbur leapt into the breach creating a Cold War curio based on Matt Cvetic, an FBI agent who infiltrated the Pittsburgh chapter of the Communist Party of the United States. By 1947, the FBI doubted Cvetic's reliability, due to arrests for disorderly behavior. But Cvetic parlayed his undercover stint into a popular radio show, and Foy bought the rights for Warner Bros. Frank Lovejoy starred in Wilbur's largely fictionalized story. In a move both unforgivable and inexplicable, the Academy nominated *I Was a Communist for the FBI* as Best Documentary of 1951. By then Cvetic had grown increasingly erratic and the FBI severed all connections with him. He lost a bid for a Republican senate seat in 1954, and the next year his son had him committed for electroshock therapy. Upon release Cvetic joined the John Birch Society and other right-wing, Christian-based crusades. He died of a heart attack waiting in line for a driver's license at the Los Angeles DMV.

The Captive City (1952)

A landmark in the changing economics and techniques of American moviemaking. Robert Wise and Mark Robson, both editors turned directors, formed Aspen Pictures to make modest movies of their own choice—and keep the profits. Their maiden effort was inspired by the US Senate's Special Committee to Investigate Organized Crime, which captivated the United States in 1951 with its televised hearings. Chaired by Democrat Estes Kefauver, it exposed organized crime's inroads into American society. Wise hired journalist Alvin Josephy Jr., veteran investigator of the rackets, to turn his experiences into a tale about a reporter (John Forsythe) exposing a small-town crime cabal. It was shot on location in Reno, using many amateur actors. Kefauver, launching a presidential bid, appeared in an on-screen prologue and epilogue. When he unexpectedly won the New Hampshire Democratic primary, incumbent president Harry Truman was forced from the race. Despite its timeliness, *The Captive City* lost money. Films copying its exposé style with bigger stars, like *The Turning Point* (1952), fared better. In Hollywood, it rarely pays to be first.

The Hitch-Hiker (1953)

Billy Cook was a petty thief whose miserable life led to a Southwest crime spree in 1950, during which he killed a traveling salesman and a family of five. *The Hitch-Hiker*, produced and directed by Ida Lupino, is based on the ordeal of James Burke and Forrest Damron, who survived an eight-day nightmare when they picked up Cook during a fishing trip in Mexico. Lupino got the hostages' story firsthand, and visited the convicted killer in San Quentin, on death row. She wanted Cook to okay the use of his name in the film. The FBI nixed it, arguing that criminals should not profit from their acts—be it through money or notoriety. Lupino and husband/coproducer, Collier Young, wrote the script, and she got career-best work from Edmond O'Brien and Frank Lovejoy as the hostages and William Talman as Cook, renamed "Emmett Myers." Despite the names being changed, many factual details remained—including the deformity that kept "Cockeyed" Cook's right eye from closing, one of the more unnerving aspects of the film. Cook, twenty-three, was executed in the gas chamber on December 12, 1952.

The Phenix City Story (1955)

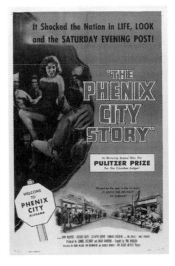

During World War II, Phenix City, Alabama (pop. 24,000), earned an outsized reputation as a den of iniquity. City fathers offered no resistance to the racket-run gambling and prostitution that became the town's economic engine. That changed on June 14, 1954, when Albert Patterson, a local lawyer who won the Democratic primary for attorney general by vowing to clean up the city, was murdered. Crane Wilbur—*who else?*—swooped in to turn Patterson's murder into a project for producer Sam Bischoff. On-location production was entrusted to Phil Karlson, who arrived in Phenix City only weeks after Patterson's death, with the killers still at large. He brazenly took cameras into the notorious 14th Street district—a haven for racketeers—and enticed locals to appear, giving the film unnerving verisimilitude. In his zeal for authenticity, Karlson dressed actor John McIntire in the actual suit Patterson was wearing when he was shot to death. Eventually a grand jury handed down 734 indictments against Phenix City cops, elected officials, and business owners who'd catered to organized crime.

The Night Holds Terror (1955)

The mid-1950s saw many home invasion hostage dramas, including *Suddenly* (1954), *Storm Fear* (1955), *The Desperate Hours* (1955), and this low-budget thriller. The main factors were Cold War–inspired insecurity that we weren't safe in our own homes, coupled with a rise in juvenile delinquency exploited in movies like *The Wild One* (1953) and *Blackboard Jungle* (1955). *The Night Holds Terror* depicts an actual 1953 incident in Lancaster, California—which also inspired *The Desperate Hours*. But this was no William Wyler show—Andrew and Virginia Stone, applying their now-patented formula, ditched the studio sets in favor of shooting *everything* on location, where events actually occurred. Gone was the classic noir look, replaced by natural sound and lighting. The Stones paid survivors Gene and Dorothy Courtier $500 for the use of their names—an idea that backfired when two of the convicted perps brought lawsuits, contending: 1) they too should have been paid, and 2) the movie ruined any hope for their rehabilitation after parole. Gene Courtier punched out one of his kidnappers in front of the jury. The judge dismissed the case—and the convicts' call for a mistrial.

While the City Sleeps (1956)

The 1953 novel *The Bloody Spur* appealed to Fritz Lang because it had echoes of his masterpiece *M* (1931). Both were based on a true crime. Between 1945 and 1946, Chicago had been terrorized by the murders of several young women. The culprit used a victim's lipstick to scrawl a plea for his capture at one murder scene. As the manhunt for the "Lipstick Killer" led nowhere, newspapers spurred the public's bloody imaginings. Hence the novel, by Chicago reporter Charles Einstein. Lang loved its mordant cynicism; reporters backstabbing each other in pursuit of the killer—not because they want justice, but because whoever

nabs the killer wins a promotion. The accused "Lipstick Killer" was seventeen-year-old William Heirens, a student at the University of Chicago who dabbled in burglary. After he was arrested near the site of one killing, police claimed his fingerprints matched those found on a note in one victim's home. Pre-Miranda, Heirens was beaten by cops and injected with "truth serum" until he confessed to one of the killings. He was charged with all three "Lipstick" murders and, on advice of lawyers, pled guilty on the promise of a life sentence instead of the chair. "I lied so I could live," he cried to the press. Case reviews were denied multiple times, and Heirens lived the rest of his life in prison. He died in 2012, at age eighty-three, maintaining his innocence to the end.

The Wrong Man (1956)

On January 14, 1953, Manny Balestrero, headed home from a regular gig at Manhattan's Stork Club, was braced by police, as he fit the description of a robbery suspect. So began his descent into the New York justice system. *The Wrong Man*, starring Henry Fonda as Balestrero, is the only Alfred Hitchcock movie closely based on a true story. In contrast to his usual style, the director went all-in for authenticity, shooting where the actual story took place, which included the cell where Manny was held and the sanitarium where his distraught wife, Rose (Vera Miles), was committed. Critics were largely dismissive, some even accusing the director of altering facts. What critics really missed was Hitchcock's usual humor. The director could usually be counted on for amusing business around the suspense, but *The Wrong Man* is unrelentingly grim. Hitchcock was angered by Warner Bros.'s insistence on a coda assuring viewers that Rose Balestrero regained her sanity. She did not. Manny sued for false arrest, getting $7,000 of the $50,000 he sought. The $22,000 Warner paid for his story all went to Rose's medical care.

I Want to Live! (1958)

A Pulitzer Prize–winning series of articles by *San Francisco Examiner* reporter Ed Montgomery provided the framework for this sensational account of the life of Barbara Graham, who on June 3, 1955, became the last woman executed in California. Graham was convicted as an accomplice in the robbery/murder of Mabel Monohan, but in jailhouse interviews with Montgomery she claimed to have been duped into it by shady cohorts. She felt her life as a hard-partying prostitute—readily related to the sympathetic reporter—prevented a fair trial. Producer Walter Wanger—who'd served time himself for wounding romantic rival Jennings Lang—hired a stellar team to tell Graham's tawdry tale. Robert Wise juiced up vestiges of his *Captive City* docudrama approach with a propulsive Johnny Mandel jazz score and a fiery performance from Susan Hayward, who'd win the Oscar for her portrayal of Graham. All previous films about capital punishment looked away from the actual execution, but *I Want to Live!* showed it in excruciating detail, making it a landmark film for that reason alone.

Susan Hayward won the 1959 Oscar for Best Actress for her portrayal of death-row inmate Barbara Graham in *I Want to Live!*

In Cold Blood (1967)

The best-selling book of 1966 related the November 15, 1959, murders of the Clutter family in Holcomb, Kansas, a "senseless" crime no one in the bucolic region could comprehend. The trauma would have remained localized if not for the arrival of two out-of-towners: Truman Capote and his colleague Harper Lee, already working on the novel *To Kill a Mockingbird* (1960), which would earn her lasting fame. Before the suspects were apprehended, Capote and Lee interviewed dozens of townsfolk and law enforcement, capturing a mosaic of Midwestern small-town life. Once killers Perry Smith and Dick Hickock were in custody, Capote had almost exclusive access to them. The resulting book (six years in the writing) was groundbreaking, not just for its novelistic approach to a true crime but for probing the lives of the killers as well as the victims. Director Richard Brooks, who also wrote the screenplay, filmed where events actually occurred—including the murder house. Conrad Hall's stunning black-and-white cinematography mixed frigid verité footage with dramatically lit scenes that played like the ghosts of film noirs past. The presence of veteran actors Paul Stewart and Charles McGraw added further reverberations of old-school noir, but Scott Wilson and Robert Blake, as Hickock and Smith (both hanged), brought a despairing depth and urgency to true crime movies never before seen. Unflinching and uncompromised, both book and film revolutionized the way such stories were told, making painful, heartbreaking "sense" of a random murder. The film culminated a year of massive change in American cinema—*Bonnie and Clyde*, *The Graduate*, *Guess Who's Coming to Dinner*, and *In the Heat of the Night* were all nominated for Best Picture—but Hollywood's old guard, desperately clinging to its reliance on reassuring entertainments, chose *Dr. Doolittle* instead of *In Cold Blood* for the final Best Picture nomination. There's no doubt, however, which film had the bigger impact on American culture. For proof, just browse any contemporary source that streams podcasts and movies. ∎

Scott Wilson and Robert Blake brought a new level of unnerving realism to their roles as disaffected killers in the stunning film version of Truman Capote's true crime classic *In Cold Blood*.

BORN

TO LOSE

DOG DAY AFTERNOON'S MANY REALITIES

By Rachel Walther

August 22, 1972: It's a muggy afternoon in Brooklyn, and three men are about to rob the Chase Manhattan Bank at the corner of Avenue P and East Third Street. They enter the lobby, wait until the last customer of the day leaves, and then things go sideways. The first man chickens out immediately and scampers off. The two remaining robbers empty the safe, only to discover that the massive take they'd anticipated isn't there. The police get tipped off,

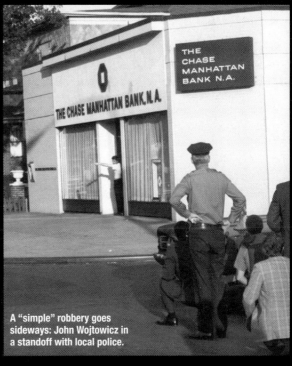

A "simple" robbery goes sideways: John Wojtowicz in a standoff with local police.

When folks got wind of the fact that Wojtowicz was robbing the bank to get money for his wife's sex-change operation, a media circus ensued.

surround the bank, and now it's cops versus robbers for the next twelve hours, with the bank workers held hostage. During the interminable wait one of the robbers asks to see his wife—when the police locate her, she turns out to be a trans woman. When news that one of the robbers is homosexual gets out, the standoff becomes a media circus, with TV cameras and onlookers flooding the neighborhood waiting for a glimpse of this guy, a mercurial and charismatic young man who's clearly in over his head. By early the next morning, the misadventure has concluded at Kennedy Airport with one robber dead and the other on his way to jail.

This is the story of both the real-life incident that occurred in 1972 and the plot of *Dog Day Afternoon*, the film based on those events that was released three years later. What brought about this strange episode in New York's history is a sensational story of transformation, rebellion, and memory; it has gone on to have a fifty-year afterlife, with both the film and the wild biography of the real-life robber, John Wojtowicz, remaining as compelling today as the when the story first broke.

"A dark, thin fellow with the broken-faced good looks of an Al Pacino or a Dustin Hoffman." — "The Boys in the Bank" by P. F. Kluge and Thomas Moore, LIFE magazine, September 22, 1972

John Wojtowicz was an average guy from Brooklyn, a straitlaced Goldwater Republican pursuing the American Dream: a wife, Carmen; two kids; saving for a house in the suburbs. His tour in Vietnam changed everything—intimate experiences in the service with other men switched on a dormant aspect of Wojtowicz's sexuality, and when he returned stateside he left Carmen, changed his politics, and began to explore the gay scene in the West Village. Wojtowicz was a strange, arrogant little guy who badgered and coaxed men into codependent relationships and campaigned doggedly for gay rights at the Gay Activist Alliance (GAA). In 1971 he met Ernest Aron, a transvestite who identified as a woman; their relationship was fraught with grievances and heated arguments, but they were committed enough to each other that when Wojtowicz proposed (despite still being married to Carmen) the two were married in November at a café in Greenwich Village. After the wedding, Aron became increasingly miserable—she was desperate for a sex change operation but couldn't afford one and was suicidal at the thought of remaining a man. Wojtowicz initially rebuffed Aron's pleas—he preferred a partner who looked like a woman but had a man's equipment—but after Aron cut her wrists the following August and ended up in the hospital, Wojtowicz vowed to get the money for the operation somewhere. He had an idea.

Wojtowicz rounded up a few guys he knew casually from around the neighborhood: Sal Naturale and Bobby Westenberg. On August 22, they psyched themselves up for the robbery by watching *The Godfather* at a theater in Times Square. Al Pacino's steely confidence in the film's final scenes, as he assumes the role of head of the Corleone family, was a swagger that Wojtowicz would imitate in the hours ahead. After they arrived at the Chase Manhattan in Brooklyn, Westenberg dropped out immediately and ran off, and Wojtowicz and Naturale were left to carry out the heist. It was a failure: the bank only had about $38,000 in cash, a much smaller take than they'd expected. The bank manager covertly signaled to a colleague over the phone that a robbery was in progress; police surrounded the bank and the two men decided to hold the workers hostage, bartering for their safe passage out of the country in exchange for the return of the employees.

They hadn't planned on hostages and didn't know what to do with them. Wojtowicz let everyone use the bathroom and allowed them to call their loved ones to let them know they were okay. The workers munched on the complimentary customer lollipops to stave off hunger; Wojtowicz ordered food for everyone from the cops outside. Folks started calling in to the bank—local law enforcement trying to ascertain the robbers' state of mind, psychos imploring Wojtowicz to "Kill them all!," and journalists eager to learn as much as possible about the situation. When asked by a reporter why he was robbing the bank, Wojtowicz explained that he needed the money to get his wife a sex-change operation, calmly stating, "[My wife's] a guy. I'm gay."

When the media got wind of this, what seemed like a "simple" bank robbery story became a cause célèbre. Networks cut in on coverage of the Republican National Convention's nomination of Richard Nixon for reelection to hover around Avenue P and Third Street, hoping to get a glimpse of Wojtowicz as he stepped outside to negotiate with the cops and to hear more about his (to many, unknown) lifestyle. Hundreds mobbed the intersection—some to jeer at the criminals but mostly to cheer on the would-be bandits and boo at the cops. At 3 a.m. the show was on the road: the FBI had secured a jet for the two men, and they rode with a handful of remaining hostages to JFK. On the tarmac, in a lightning-fast confrontation Naturale was shot by the FBI and Wojtowicz was taken into custody. For the hostages, their nightmare was over—for Wojtowicz, a new reality was just beginning.

LIFE magazine ran a feature on the incident next month, recounting the "bizarre" details of Wojtowicz's marriage to Aron as well as focusing on the hapless but relatively humane treatment the two men provided to their captives and the Us versus Them attitude that spread out from the bank and onto the televisions of the East Coast: "After all, the robbers and the hostages are in this together, but the determined men outside are strangers."

"It took on its own life." —Al Pacino

Martin Bregman was a talent agent who aspired to produce motion pictures. He read "The Boys in the Bank" and saw potential, a project that he could develop and build around his star client, Al Pacino. He enlisted Frank Pierson, who'd scripted *Cool Hand Luke* (1967), to write the screenplay, and tasked Sidney Lumet to direct. After several unsuccessful attempts to meet with Wojtowicz in prison, Pierson opted instead to fashion an image of his main character, renamed Sonny Wortzik, based on interviews with anyone and everyone Wojtowicz had come in contact with. The more he spoke to people, the blurrier Pierson's notion of Wojtowicz became: "Everyone knew a different person and described a different person." To Carmen, John was the model husband—a good provider and affectionate father; to Ernest Aron, he was volatile and dangerous; to the Brooklyn crowd on August 22, he was a charming ring-

John Cazale (left) and Al Pacino (right) were old friends in real life, playing two wage-slave losers getting to know each other over the course of the robbery.

leader. The one common thread for the screenwriter among all these disparate reports was Wojtowicz's desire to take care of everyone, to be who others needed him to be. It was this trait that he used to build Sonny, a sympathetic loser in over his head with the number of responsibilities he's saddled himself with, on the verge of snapping under the strain of managing the endless needs of his loved ones.

Pacino initially balked at the project. He was exhausted from months of nonstop shooting on *The Godfather Part II* (1974) and remembered that working with Lumet the year before on *Serpico* (1973) was rewarding but arduous. And, as the director would reflect years later: "No major American star that I know of had ever played a role like this." *Dog Day Afternoon* would be pushing the envelope, the first mainstream film to center around a gay character since the film adaptation of the successful 1968 play *The Boys in the Band* five years earlier. But while that film was a harrowing drama focused on questions of sexual identity and self-acceptance, here was an action thriller comedy with a gay antihero. Would audiences accept Sonny? Bregman explains the mindset behind the story's development: "[These guys] were normal human beings, with human emotions, in a bizarre setting. We didn't show them as freaks because we never considered them freaks." After reading Pierson's final script, Pacino reconsidered: here was role that was complex and sympathetic, volatile yet humane. And if he said no, Dustin Hoffman might snap it up.

The next key element was casting Sal Naturale (Pierson retained his first name in the script). The real Sal was just eighteen, an angry kid with a troubled past filled with juvenile detention centers and abuse. Since they'd be acting in lockstep with one another in nearly every scene, Lumet insisted that Pacino sit in on auditions; after dozens of maybes, Pacino suggested his friend John Cazale, with whom he'd just finished shooting Coppola's epic. The slight, balding actor seemed all wrong for the role of the violent yet angelic Sal—until Cazale read for the part. Within two lines, Lumet was sold

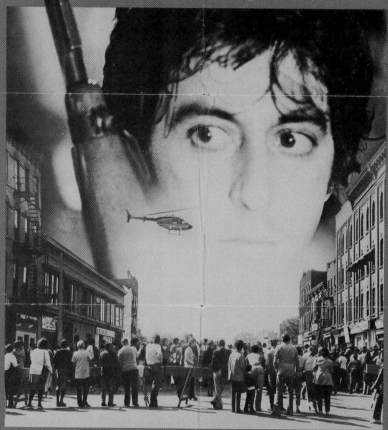

on Pacino's suggestion, and the two actors would craft a partnership on-screen that was the antithesis of what they'd just achieved in *The Godfather Part II*. Michael and Fredo Corleone are bonded by blood and weighed down with decades-long resentments and betrayals; in Lumet's film they are practically strangers, wage-slave losers betting double or nothing on an impossible dream.

The circus of August 22, 1972, was rivaled only by two months' shooting in Park Slope. Lumet insisted on three weeks of rehearsal before filming began, and rather than asking the supporting players cast as the bank workers to imitate the actual captives, the actors were encouraged to dress in their own clothes and stretch and rework Pierson's scripted lines to suit their own vernacular. This process forged a bond among the cast and aided their sense of familiarity on-screen. Cinematographer Victor Kemper utilized natural or naturally present artificial lighting for every scene, to strip any element of stylization from the action; Lumet also eschewed a music score of any kind, explaining: "It was so important to me that an audience believe that it really happened because what happened was so outrageous." A general call for extras to fill out the crowd grew each successive evening, with up to 3,000 locals turning out every night to watch the show and become a part of it.

The film's mordant humor came from everywhere: reports from the hostages in Kluge and Moore's original article, Pierson's script, Lumet's extensive rehearsals, and in-the-moment improvisations. According to Kluge and Moore, bank manager Robert Barrett told Wojtowicz, "I'm supposed to hate you guys, but I've had more laughs tonight than I've had in weeks." Pacino's difficulty in opening a gift box in which his shotgun is concealed during the film's first moments was an on-screen accident that hints at other unintentionally funny moments to come. In a scene where Sonny tells Sal that the FBI is furnishing them with a jet to leave the United States, he asks his friend where he might like to go. Cazale gives a considerate pause be-

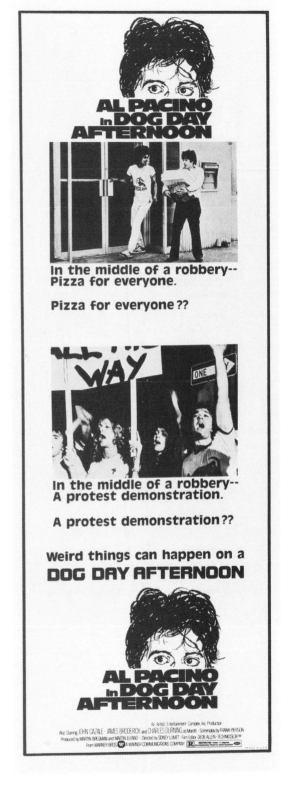

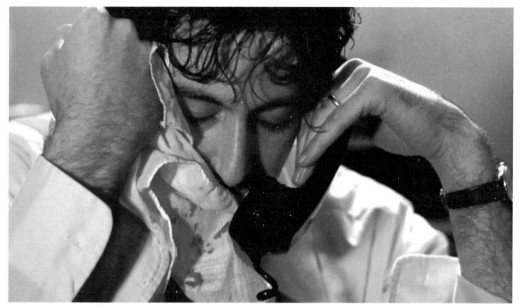

Pacino's Sonny Wortzik is a volatile live wire who confronts instant fame and the prospect of losing everything over the course of one hot summer night.

fore solemnly replying: "Wyoming," a line improvised by the actor. Lumet chose newcomer Chris Sarandon to play Leon, the character based on Aron, and while Sarandon and Pacino never meet on camera their long, plaintive phone call to each other is heartrending and poignant, with lines derived from Pierson's interviews with Aron as well as Lumet's incisive note to Sarandon during his audition: "Less Blanche DuBois, more Queens housewife."

"What happened then was either more or less than the robbers deserved." — Kluge and Moore, "The Boys in the Bank"

Lumet's concern about the audience's reaction to Sonny was unfounded. Thanks to the respectful treatment of his relationship with Leon, and the realistic foundation the film had achieved by enhancing the natural whenever possible, *Dog Day Afternoon* was a smash hit with audiences and critics. It touched on not only the underrepresented topic of gay life in the 1970s, but also the transformative glare of the media spotlight that conflated infamy with fame in the pursuit of ratings. (Lumet's next film, *Network* [1976], built on that theme to a crescendo of satire and terror.) The film was nominated for six Academy Awards for Best Picture, Best Director, Best Actor, Best Original Screenplay, Best Supporting Actor, and Best Editing, and Pierson won for his script (the film had the misfortune of competing against *One Flew over the Cuckoo's Nest* [1975], which swept the ceremony).

A breakthrough role in the portrayal of a gay man in mainstream film belied a more complex reality. Many in the gay community, particularly those in GAA, saw Wojtowicz's criminal behavior and theatrics as a severe hindrance to their cause. They did not want this macho, foul-mouthed live wire representing them and their movement. When Wojtowicz returned to the Brooklyn branch of Chase Manhattan in the late 1970s with a news crew to sign autographs and pose for photos in a shirt that said "I ROBBED THIS BANK," teller and former hostage Santa Strazella bitterly remarked: "[He's] signing autographs and becoming a big star—making money on an ordeal he put a lot of people through."

While Wojtowicz failed to achieve his original goal in the robbery, he succeeded in selling that failure to Hollywood. While the total amount he received from Warner Bros. was determined privately after decades of litigation, he used the initial $7,500 advance sent to him in 1975 to pay for Aron's

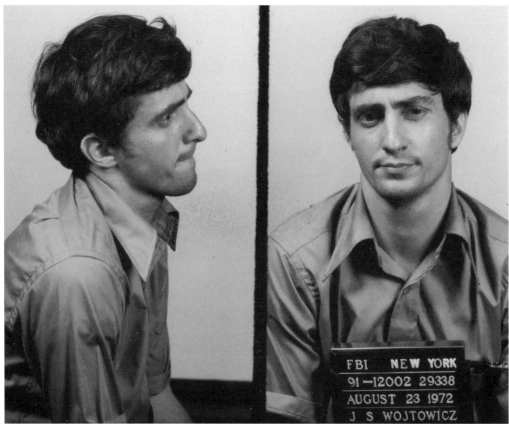

Wojtowicz's mugshot, the day one reality ended for him and a new one began.

Aron's gender reassignment surgery. Aron changed her name to Liz Eden, cut all ties with her husband, and eventually moved to upstate New York. In prison, Wojtowicz's status as a celebrity criminal saved him from abuse in some cases and fostered it in others—Pierson's invented subplot that Sonny may or may not have been complicit with the FBI in serving up Sal to their gunfire branded the real-life robber a rat. After the film was shown at Lewisburg Prison, Wojtowicz was attacked several times. Through a series of legal maneuvers he got his sentence reduced; when he was released in April 1978 he tried to make up for his unemployable status as an ex-con by cashing in on his enduring fame, nicknaming himself "The Dog" and explaining to anyone within earshot his pivotal relationship to the film. Wojtowicz even applied to work as a security guard at Chase Manhattan, explaining to them that "Nobody's gonna rob The Dog's bank."

After the success of *Dog Day Afternoon*, Pacino's winning streak ended with *Bobby Deerfield* (1977), a languid romance about a race car driver's doomed affair with a fatally ill socialite that tanked at the box office. In *Cruising* (1980), his portrayal of a naive cop who goes undercover in lower Manhattan's S&M gay subculture pushed the envelope further than the role of Sonny, but the film's uneven plot, protests during the film's production by gay activist groups, and Pacino's clashes with director William Friedkin branded the film as notorious rather than entertaining and it became hard to find in subsequent decades. Over the next twenty years, Pacino went on to finally net an Oscar (for *Scent of a Woman* [1992]) and achieve cult-film immortality as Tony Montana in Brian De Palma's *Scarface* (1983), but his credits since 1975 inspired him to remark to biographer Lawrence Grobel in 2009: "I haven't made a good film since *Dog Day Afternoon*."

As for the real bank employees, they returned to work and went on with their lives, never forgetting

August 1972. Josephine Tutino, a teller haunted by the ordeal, worked through her trauma by writing the song "Lollipops & Shotguns (A Hostage's Lament)," which her husband had privately recorded. The resulting pop song transcends novelty and is a bona fide swinger, with backup singers and the catchy (if macabre) hook, "Eating lollipops with shotguns aimed at your eyes / Eating lollipops with danger at your side." As Tutino recalled years later, "I had to write it down just to get it out of me."

"I'm the bank robber, fuck Al Pacino."
—John Wojtowicz

In the twenty-first century, a new generation of filmmakers, raised on *Dog Day Afternoon*, approached Wojtowicz and asked him for his story. Wojtowicz was as mercurial and difficult as ever, demanding that callers ask to speak with The Dog, not John, and railing about Warner Bros.'s continued reluctance to pay him his full share of the film's profits. French media artist Pierre Huyghe endured Wojtowicz's eccentricities to create *The Third Memory* (2000), a short film in which Wojtowicz returns to a studio-build replica of the bank (tellingly it's the film's fictional First Brooklyn Savings Bank, not the real Chase Manhattan branch) and directs the action and narrates what everyone did and said on that fateful day. The resulting ten-minute film displays how much Wojtowicz's memory of the events is infected with scenes from Lumet's film, and every aspect of that day's action in his mind's eye paints him as a romantic hero deeply wronged (he argues, contrary to other eyewitnesses' accounts, that Sal was murdered by FBI agents in cold blood after he had been disarmed, yet shows no remorse at the pivotal role he played in his friend's untimely death). Huyghe explained: "[My film] is not the memory of the event. John has no memory of the event, to be honest. And it's not the memory that he's built from all the media. It's what he creates, he takes a part of each thing and makes his own, new memory."

In the Dutch documentary *Based on a True Story* (2004), Richard Wandel, former president of GAA, puts it more succinctly: "I'm sure John to this day thinks of himself as quite a hero. But I think he's just foolish.... He still hasn't figured out what it's all about." Director Walter Stokman's film, like Pierson's mosaic of Wojtowicz, interviews many of the people involved with the incident besides The Dog, whose serpentine mind games with the filmmaker and demands for high sums over the phone are laced over contradictory impressions of that day from tellers, FBI agent James Murphy, and archival footage of Liz Eden. (Eden was not interviewed for the film, as she succumbed to AIDS in 1987.) Wojtowicz was finally interviewed at length in *The Dog* (2013), a thorough portrait of the man's life by Allison Berg and Frank Keraudren that displays his bravado, charm, and fuzzy relationship to the truth; it also depicts his fight with cancer, a struggle that claimed Wojtowicz in 2009. Wojtowicz's children did not participate in either documentary; his ex-wife Carmen explains that their son, Sean, wants nothing to do with his father. But, Sean's favorite movie star? Al Pacino.

"You gotta get fun out of life."
—Sonny Wortzik

Dog Day Afternoon's themes of alienation, LGBTQ+ life, gender identity, and media madness read like a treatment for a script currently in production rather than a film approaching its fiftieth birthday. Despite its heavy topics, its success lies in the fact that the story is anything but—it's also an entertaining heist film about love, community, and acceptance. Pacino's Sonny Wortzik may not have been an exact duplication of John Wojtowicz, but who was Wojtowicz exactly during those moments in the bank, with Pacino's line "I'll make him an offer he can't refuse" still ringing in his head? The pieces will never match up, but the myriad realities of August 22, 1972, continue to loop in a möbius strip that is endlessly compelling. ∎

Born to Lose is being expanded to a book, forthcoming from Headpress in 2025.

BURDEN OF PROOF

COLD CASE NOIR

By Danilo Castro

Hollywood has always been at odds with the truth. Studios love capitalizing on the public's interest in real-life stories by adapting them for the big screen, but as we all know, real life is too complicated to fit a three-act structure. Concessions are made, whether it be in the form of an imagined character or a shuffling of historical events to reach a more dramatic conclusion. As long as the reshaped story bears a resemblance to what actually happened, and the fictionalized elements are entertaining, studios assume that audiences will be satisfied.

Satisfaction becomes elusive, however, when the real-life story has no conclusion. There have been numerous attempts to make films about unsolved crimes, but the thing that makes these cases appealing in theory is the very thing that makes them difficult to adapt. They invalidate the three-act structure. They provide a tantalizing premise without any of the payoff. These films—let's call them "cold case adaptations"—have been especially prevalent in the twenty-first century, and what makes them worthy of discussion is that each takes a different approach to the same narrative challenge. They use the negative space afforded them to develop an even more ambiguous style of noir.

The murder of Elizabeth Short inspired other books and films besides Ellroy's *The Black Dahlia*. *True Confessions* (1981, above) recreated the infamous crime scene, as did the 1975 TV movie *Who Is the Black Dahlia?* (directed by noir veteran Joe Pevney), in which Lucy Arnaz played the ill-fated Short.

Of these cold case adaptations, *The Black Dahlia* (2006) has the most complicated relationship with the truth. The film is based on the James Ellroy novel of the same name, which in turn is based on the grisly murder of Elizabeth Short. The well-known details, including the discovery of Short's body in a vacant lot and the media circus that ensued, are accurately portrayed. The investigation that follows, however, takes a lot of creative liberties, most notably finding a culprit for that infamous crime in January 1947.

The real Elizabeth Short waited tables and lived off of Hollywood Boulevard. The fictional Short (Mia Kirshner) is at the fulcrum of Hollywood decadence, making stag films and fraternizing with old money when she isn't performing humiliating screen tests. *The Black Dahlia* makes no bones about which version is more scintillating, both for the viewer and the fictional detectives assigned to the case. Dwight "Bucky" Bleichert (Josh Hartnett) and Lee Blanchard (Aaron Eckhart) become so obsessed with

The film's scandalized depiction of Elizabeth Short (above) has little in common with the real woman (below).

Short that perverse side effects take root in their personal lives. The former romances a Short lookalike, while the latter turns abusive toward his longtime girlfriend.

Blurring the lines between fact and fiction is not inherently a bad thing. Ellroy's novel is a brilliant mashup of pulp and tabloid myths, and the film follows suit. At least, it tries to. The original cut ran three hours, with screen time dedicated to real-life figures like Marjorie Graham and Robert "Red" Manley, as well as the psychological toll the case takes on Bleichert over several years. Universal Pictures demanded it be whittled down to 120 minutes, which meant condensing the plot and scrapping the aforementioned characters. The studio also emphasized the tagline "inspired by true events" during the film's promotion. Director Brian De Palma took issue with both of these decisions. In his estimation, they created a disconnect between what film audiences got and what they *thought* they were getting.

I'm not here to reclaim *The Black Dahlia* as some lost masterpiece. It's a mess, and it's hard to imagine a longer runtime would have smoothed over the terrible lead performances and stilted presentation. I will point to the climax, however, as an example of something the film gets right. Bleichert forces a confession out of deranged socialite Ramona Linscott (Fiona Shaw), but she shoots herself before he can make the arrest. The detective can't prove a thing, and the Short case remains officially unsolved. It's a seminal noir wrinkle, and a clever way of rewriting history while maintaining the same, bleak outcome.

Hollywoodland **(2006)** is about a person trying to rewrite history in real time. Louis Simo (Adrien Brody) is a private detective who's more than willing to fabricate a headline if it means a few more bucks in his pocket. He looks into the death of *Adventures of Superman* star George Reeves (Ben Affleck) despite it being ruled a suicide, and the first thing he does is sidle up to the press and spread rumors of foul play. It's 1959, still the Golden Age of celebrity gossip. The kicker, of course, is that the more Simo digs up about the actor, the more the detective comes to believe his own press.

Simo is based on celebrity gumshoe–author Milo Speriglio, and the decision to tell the story from his perspective gives *Hollywoodland* a basis in reality. The operative word here being *basis*. Simo doesn't have a shred of evidence, but his tenacity, coupled with the bizarre circumstances in which Reeves's body was found, make for an admittedly persuasive argument. Why were there no fingerprints on the actor's gun? Why were there bullet holes in the floor of his bedroom? The police officers handling the case fail to provide satisfying answers, much like their real-life counterparts. They'd rather maintain the status quo than rock the boat of powerful studio executives like Eddie Mannix (Bob Hoskins).

Simo hits the same roadblocks. His investigation leads to skirmishes with Reeves's fiancée, Leonore Lemmon (Robin Tunney), and his former mistress, Toni Mannix (Diane Lane), now married to the aforementioned exec. Their fraught relationships with the actor are shown through increasingly dismal flashbacks. The film is at its best during these passages, carefully building motives for each of the characters while presenting Reeves as an imperfect charmer. He was a superhero who couldn't seem to figure out life as a regular guy. Simo winds up having the opposite problem. He gets a chance to patch things

Ben Affleck was cast as George Reeves after scheduling conflicts forced the studio's original choice, Hugh Jackman, to drop out.

Simo (Adrien Brody) may be based on Milo Speriglio, but the character is significantly older, and his troubled personal life is invented for the film.

up with his estranged son (a Superman fan, naturally), but he doesn't get to break open the case in heroic fashion. He still believes it's foul play, he just can't figure out what kind.

The film can't, either. Instead of extrapolating a conclusion, *Hollywoodland* goes the multiple-choice route, presenting three different versions of Reeves's death: accidental shooting by Lemmon, murder by one of Mannix's goons, and suicide. These scenarios are well staged by director Allen Coulter, and each is given the necessary context to be convincing. The decision to end with the actor's suicide, however, gives the film an unexpected poignancy. Reeves was so closely tied to the role of Superman it became his albatross. Having failed to get a production company off the ground, he was faced with having to put the tights back on shortly before his death. He was forty-five years old. It's telling that after two hours of proposed coverups, the simplest possibility is still the most tragic.

A decade after Reeves's death and a few hundred miles away, the Zodiac Killer began his reign of terror. The Zodiac transfixed the San Francisco Bay Area between 1968 and 1974, killing five people and taunting local newspapers with ciphers that supposedly revealed his identity. He threatened to shoot out the tires of school buses and the students on them unless his ciphers were published. David Fincher was one of these students. The future director was tailed by squad cars and told of the Zodiac's high-powered rifle by his dad, which may have sparked his career-long fascination with serial killers. Fincher briefly considered directing *The Black Dahlia*, but **Zodiac** (2007) gave him the rare opportunity to meld personal experience with formal precision, and the result was a genre-defining masterpiece.

The film's adherence to fact is exemplary. Fincher and screenwriter James Vanderbilt spent eighteen months researching the case to make sure that every crucial detail was accounted for. The only crimes depicted are the ones with surviving witnesses, and a different actor plays the Zodiac each time, to better illustrate the discrepancies that existed in the police descriptions. The friendship between *San Francisco Chronicle* cartoonist Robert Graysmith (Jake Gyllenhaal) and reporter Paul Avery (Robert Downey Jr.) is the biggest creative liberty taken, as the two men rarely crossed paths in their professional life. Their scenes are so important to the film's conceit, however, that I'm inclined to give it a pass. Graysmith and Avery bond over the case and are subsequently broken by it, with the former descending into obsession and the latter drinking himself into oblivion.

Graysmith's compulsiveness is introduced as a boyish quirk. He's late submitting a cartoon because he tries to solve one of the Zodiac's ciphers. Avery mocks him, and SFPD inspector Dave Toschi

The production had trees flown in via helicopter to make sure the Lake Berryessa murder site looked exactly like it did in 1969.

(Mark Ruffalo) barely knows who he is. He even manages to charm his future wife, Melanie (Chloë Sevigny), by turning their first date into part of the investigation. The second half of *Zodiac* probes Graysmith's dark side. As more time passes and the police involved with the case either retire or get reassigned, the more fanatically determined Graysmith becomes. He wakes up Toschi in the middle of the night with new leads and pursues suspects that were dismissed years earlier. Threatening phone calls do little to deter him from writing his own book about the case (upon which the film is based). *Zodiac* threads the needle between subjectivity and objectivity; the viewer is compelled enough to share Graysmith's curiosity but removed enough to fear the consequences of his actions.

Graysmith tracks down his prime suspect, Arthur Leigh Allen (John Carroll Lynch), in the film's

Brad Pitt and Daniel Craig were considered for the role of Paul Avery before Robert Downey Jr. (left) was cast. Jake Gyllenhaal (right) was the first choice for Robert Graysmith.

penultimate scene. He looks Allen in the eye, lingers for a moment, and then walks away. No arrest, no confession, no catharsis. *Zodiac* doesn't know who its titular killer is, and it defies other cold case adaptations by turning this ambiguity into a dramatic strength. The tension doesn't come from a clever twist, but from wondering how many years of their lives Graysmith and Toschi will sacrifice before finally calling it a day. "Do you know more people die in the East Bay commute every three months than that idiot ever killed?" The question, posed by Avery, sums up the futility of the whole affair. Fincher may have modeled his film on *All the President's Men* (1976), but in depicting the failed efforts of real-life people, *Zodiac* assumes a worldview far more nihilistic—and far more noir—than its predecessor.

Memories of Murder (2003) was linked to *Zodiac* before either film existed. The former is based on the Hwaseong serial murders that occurred between 1986 and 1991, and the culprit behind them was referred

STRANGER THAN FICTION

Cold cases are more popular than ever. You'd be hard-pressed to find an unsolved murder that hasn't been extensively covered by a podcast or a documentary miniseries. That being said, no coverage has been as bizarre or as revelatory as that of Robert Durst. The son of a New York real estate magnate, Durst was a suspect in three different crimes: the disappearance of his wife, Kathleen McCormack, in 1982, the murder of his friend Susan Berman in 2000, and the death of his neighbor Morris Black in 2001.

All Good Things (2010) dramatizes these crimes, and the conspicuous ways in which Durst avoided punishment. The film changes the names of those involved—including Durst, who becomes David Marks (Ryan Gosling)—but the rest of the story is based on case files and interviews director Andrew Jarecki conducted with Durst's associates. *All Good Things* is an engaging thriller, its most notable attribute being its refusal to give a definitive take on what happened. This tact was noted by Durst of all people, who sang Jarecki's praises and even recorded a commentary with the director for the film's DVD release.

Durst's comfort with Jarecki, a documentarian by trade, was unprecedented. The millionaire had never discussed his personal life, and yet he agreed to star in the documentary miniseries *The Jinx: The Life and Deaths of Robert Durst* (2015) as a means of dispelling his lurid reputation. Instead, the miniseries confirmed it. Durst's interviews with Jarecki, which were conducted over several years, present a disquieting and unreliable figure. He admits to fabricating an alibi the night his wife disappeared, and he's shockingly cavalier about the fact that he was accused of murdering Black while pretending to be a mute woman named Dorothy Ciner.

The Jinx moves through its six episodes with verve. The nonlinear structure and the flashy opening credits make it clear that the show aims to entertain, but never at the expense of its serious subject matter. In the finale, Jarecki confronts Durst with newly discovered evidence, and the millionaire is visibly flummoxed. Durst excuses himself to use the restroom and, forgetting his microphone is still on, mumbles the words: "What the hell did I do? Killed them all, of course." It's a jaw-dropping moment, a genuine instance of reality proving stranger than fiction. Durst tried to walk back his comment afterward, but the damage had been done. He was charged with Berman's murder and arrested the day before the episode aired. He was sentenced to life in prison in 2021, where he would die the following year.

Durst prompting his own downfall is dramatic irony at its finest, but even more incredible is the fact that Jarecki leveraged a film without a resolution into a miniseries that provided one. He recontextualized his own cold case adaptation by solving the case. It's such a singular achievement that any survey of true crime in which the director isn't mentioned is incomplete.

—Danilo Castro

FROM **BONG JOON HO** ACADEMY AWARD®
WINNING DIRECTOR OF **PARASITE**

MEMORIES OF MURDER

Detectives Park (Song Kang-ho, left) and Seo (Kim Sang-kyung, right). Kim slept fewer hours during production to give his character a haggard appearance.

to as the "Korean Zodiac Killer." Bong Joon-ho was intrigued by the country's decision to ape Western iconography, and the writer-director explores this uneasy dynamic throughout the film. Characters are constantly referencing US shows and parroting English phrases. In one crucial instance, the police are forced to send evidence to the United States because they don't have the technology to process it themselves. *Memories of Murder* takes on the same cold case themes as its peers, but the decision to frame them as symptoms of a stifled, autocratic government provides a rich subtext.

The Hwaseong police are doomed from the start, and their inexperience can be gleaned from the differing methods of their detectives. Park Doo-man (Song Kang-ho) vows to find the killer through intuition. He prides himself on being able to tell if a man is guilty by simply looking him in the eye. Seo Tae-yoon (Kim Sang-kyung) values facts, and is quick to rule out a suspect if he doesn't check all the boxes. The film charts the slow, agonizing realization that neither method is working. Park's instincts lead to the wrong man being charged, and when he runs out of easy targets, he resorts to magic potions to summon the killer. Seo has promising theories, but his discipline breaks down when he tries to shoot a suspect whose DNA results are inconclusive. Park stops him, signifying a breaking point of his own. He is forced to consider, for the first time, whether any of it matters.

The epilogue is a chilling embodiment of the film's title. It's 2003 and Park has changed careers. An impromptu visit to the first crime scene leads to him being told that another man recently made the same pilgrimage. The man was apparently reminiscing on something he did long ago, and upon hearing this, Park reverts to his old self. He turns toward the camera and stares, desperate for more information. The film has none to offer, however. Fade to black. Once more, a director finds a novel way to address the unresolved. Breaking the fourth wall allows Bong to pass the burden of proof onto the viewer, so we must continue to ask questions after the credits roll. Unless, of course, the viewer has something to hide. Bong was certain the actual Korean Zodiac Killer would see *Memories of Murder*, and he wanted an ending that would make him feel seen in return. The killer was going to look Park in the eye, whether he liked it or not.

Bong was right. Lee Choon-jae confessed to the Hwaseong serial murders in 2019, after his DNA was linked to one of the victims. He could not be prosecuted for the murders due to the statute of limitations, but he was already serving a life sentence for killing his sister-in-law in 1994. Lee was given the chance to watch *Memories of Murder* during a 2020 court case, and while his response was predictably sociopathic ("I had no feelings or emotions toward the movie"), there's a satisfaction in knowing that the director reached his intended target. Justice was belatedly served. *Memories of Murder* is the rare cold case adaptation that's been solved after the fact, but it has not been diminished as a result. If anything, the film's predictive storytelling has allowed it to play better now than when it was originally released.

The Black Dahlia, *Hollywoodland*, *Zodiac*, and *Memories of Murder* were released in the span of five years, and their respective approaches can be summarized as: fiction, speculation, dramatization, and manifestation. They were by no means the first, but in surveying the last decade of cold case films, the quartet proves useful as a template. *The Irishman* (2019) spun a fictional narrative around the disappearance of Jimmy Hoffa, and despite receiving criticism from Hoffa scholars, the film earned ten Oscar nominations. *Boston Strangler* (2023) was a blatant *Zodiac* homage, right down to the period setting and the protagonist being a journalist, while *The Night of the 12th* (2022) won six César Awards for its Bongian depiction of an unsolved murder.

In the original film noir era, endings were mostly decisive. The killer is put behind bars, the crook botches the heist, the femme fatale gets blown away. The cold case noir takes it a step further by proposing the only thing worse than tragedy: uncertainty. We're wired as moviegoers to make sense of the mysteries laid out before us, so when the opportunity to do so is removed, our deepest anxieties fill the void and our desire to learn the truth grows tenfold. The films discussed here reconcile these contradictory feelings, and in doing so, they say more about the human condition than a proper conclusion ever could. ■

Jean Hagen on the set of *Side Street* (1949).

Tony Curtis in *Sweet Smell of Success* (1957).

Louis Hayward and Joan Leslie in *Repeat Performance* (1947).

Scott Wilson and Robert Blake in *In Cold Blood* (1967).

Andrew Robinson and Walter Matthau in *Charley Varrick* (1973).

Akim Tamiroff and Orson Welles in *Touch of Evil* (1958).

GUNS FOR HIRE

A CHRONOLOGICAL SURVEY OF THE HIT MAN IN FILM NOIR

Danilo Castro

The hit man is a quintessential film noir character. He specializes in murder and looks sharp in the process. He isn't weighed down by the dutiful obligations of police officers, or the moral scruples of private eyes, and he gets paid more than either. He will assuredly wind up six feet under, however. The hit man never lives long, and what time he does have is spent in isolation, often fighting the nagging fear that he's made a terrible career choice. It's easier to contend with a bullet from a rival gun than a guilty conscience.

These qualities have allowed the hit man to thrive in every era of noir. The character is distinct enough to be instantly recognizable, yet broad enough to allow filmmakers and actors to bring their own interpretations to the table. The twenty films comprising this survey come with a few ground rules because rules are crucial to the hit man ethos: no political assassins, government agents, or serial killers allowed. Those men kill for reasons other than money, while our focus is on working-class fellows who couldn't care less about the "who" and "why" of it all. They pull triggers to make ends meet. They'd likely be incensed by the light this piece shines on them, but such are the risks we take here at *NOIR CITY*.

THIS GUN FOR HIRE (1942)

The hit man was never supposed to be the star. Paramount purchased the rights to Graham Greene's novel *A Gun for Sale* in 1936, and when it came time to adapt it for the big screen as *This Gun for Hire*, the man playing the titular gun was given fourth billing. We'd seen passionate gangsters and reluctant outlaws before, but spotlighting someone who killed for money seemed a commercially risky proposition. The public loved it. Philip Raven became a cultural sensation, catapulting Alan Ladd to superstardom (he was given an "introducing" credit despite having acted for ten years). Raven established a cinematic template for the hit man that's still in use today; his trench coat and fedora combination became standard issue, as did the character's sociopathic bent. It's the brief flashes of empathy, however, that make the character so effective. Raven's friendship with nightclub singer Ellen Graham (Veronica Lake) and his unfailing kindness toward kittens hint at the hurt and bitterness lurking within. Raven's struggle to reconcile with this humanity is so well executed that it holds up after eight decades of emulation.

Alan Ladd was cast in *This Gun for Hire* at the urging of talent agent Sue Carol, who also happened to be his wife.

ASSASSIN FOR HIRE (1951)

This Gun for Hire proved a tough act to follow. It took Hollywood more than a decade to depict another contract killer. In the interim, *Assassin for Hire* was released by British studio Anglo-Amalgamated, and though largely forgotten, the film provides one of the earliest examples of a hit man afflicted by a guilty conscience. Antonio Riccardi (Sydney Tafler) is an Italian immigrant who moonlights as a professional killer in order to pay for his brother's violin lessons. After he carries out what appears to be a routine assignment, a series of mishaps lead Riccardi to believe that he may have shot his own brother by mistake. *Assassin for Hire* features some evocative set pieces courtesy of director Michael McCarthy, and a lead performance admirably committed to upending the "cool" hit man persona, but the finale is where the film's strengths coalesce. A distraught Riccardi confesses to the police, only to be told that his brother is alive and well. The whole mix-up was a sting operation, and Riccardi gets booked for killing the right man. Karma, thy name is noir.

NEW YORK CONFIDENTIAL (1955)

Contract killing is an inherently lonely vocation. Assassins share as little as possible, and want to know even less about their employers. *New York Confidential*, the sixth collaboration between screenwriters Russell Rouse and Clarence Greene, details what happens when a hit man gets too close with a mob family and the line between friends, lovers, and enemies becomes irrevocably tangled. The film doesn't chart a linear progression from professional to personal, but rather a string of bad decisions and double-crosses that shift the alliances of characters from one moment to the next. Rouse, who also directs, takes great care to depict Nick Magellan (Richard Conte) as a man being gradually worn down by obligation. In the finale, Magellan is ordered to silence his boss, Charlie Lupo (Broderick Crawford), and his decision to linger at the crime scene undermines the professional detachment he'd previously shown on the job. He's past the point of no return. The fact that Magellan is gunned down moments later seems almost superfluous—by that point the mob is simply putting a walking corpse out of its misery.

THE LINEUP (1958)

The hit men in the 1940s and early 1950s were bad men in the "Hollywood" sense, which is to say they had virtuous qualities and inner conflicts that made their sins palatable on-screen. *The Lineup* is a watershed release because it was among the first films to ditch the safety net of likeability and depict hit men as deranged lunatics. The film is ostensibly about a police manhunt to bring hit man partners Dancer (Eli Wallach) and Julian (Robert Keith) to justice. The duo is turning San Francisco upside down in an attempt to recover a shipment

Bob Bailey (left) and Eli Wallach as handler and hitman in *The Lineup*.

of smuggled heroin, and they're leaving a trail of mangled corpses in their wake. *The Lineup* is based on the TV series of the same name, but director Don Siegel and screenwriter Stirling Silliphant blow open the constraints of the small screen with visceral, unrelentingly violent set pieces. There are no appeals to the basic decency of the viewer; there are only shootouts—including one in which Dancer uses a child as a human shield. *The Lineup* flopped upon initial release, but its hard-nosed attitude has resurfaced in everything from Bob Dylan lyrics to Siegel's other Bay Area classic, *Dirty Harry* (1971).

MURDER BY CONTRACT (1958)

Discipline and preparation are part of the hit man's appeal. There's an insidious thrill in watching a criminal formulate a plan and stick to it, especially when the stakes are life or death. *Murder by Contract* distills this thrill down into its 81-minute runtime. The protagonist is a familiar type: a clinical, precise hit man named Claude (Vince Edwards). The difference here is that director Irving Lerner applies the same clinical precision to the storytelling. The character and the form are so integrated they move as one, allowing for an elliptical style that has more in common with the burgeoning French New Wave than other B-movies being released in this period. The barbershop sequence, in which Claude executes his first contract, doesn't contain a drop of blood, yet its measured pacing and suggestive inserts make it one of the most sinister kills ever orchestrated. It's rivaled by the disturbingly intimate POV shots that distinguish the finale. *Murder by Contract* showed that overt exposition and moral condemnation weren't necessary in a film about a hired killer. Audiences could simply tune in to the character's wavelength and figure the rest out for themselves.

BLAST OF SILENCE (1961)

Hollywood was changing in the late 1950s and early 1960s. DIY filmmakers like Paul Wendkos, Stanley Kubrick, and the aforementioned Lerner were shooting in actual locations without permits, and achieving a level of gritty verisimilitude that informed the last wave of the original noir era as well as the first wave of neo-noir. Allen Baron was a comic book artist by trade who decided to transfer his sequential storytelling technique to the movie screen with *Blast of Silence*. The result was a micro-budget masterpiece. Baron plays Frankie Bono, a Cleveland hit man who travels to New York City during Christmas to punch a guy's ticket. He glimpses the possibility of a better life while reconnecting with childhood friends, but the demands of the job and a few crucial missteps resign him to a watery grave. Baron's direction is remarkably assured for a novice, and his background as an illustrator manifests in a series of frames that manage to be both gorgeous and desolate. *Blast of Silence* is as bleak as holiday viewing gets, but the unique, second-person narration by Lionel Stander gives the film an undercurrent of black comedy. There's nothing else quite like it. [Read more about *Blast of Silence* in Jeremy Arnold's article on page 122.]

Allen Baron only played the role of the doomed hitman in *Blast of Silence* because Peter Falk turned it down.

THE KILLERS (1964)

The 1946 version of *The Killers* opens with arguably the most iconic hit man sequence of all time. Max (William Conrad) and Al (Charles McGraw) emerge from the shadows into a small-town diner, harass the staff for the whereabouts of "the Swede," and disappear after closing the book, guns blazing, on the doomed ex-boxer. If they stuck around for more than ten minutes, they'd be guaranteed a spot on the list of cinema's most colorful killers. Eighteen years later, Don Siegel's version of *The Killers* promoted the hit men, renamed Charlie (Lee Marvin) and Lee (Clu Gulager), from secondary players to protagonists. Curious as to why the marked man didn't run from his fate, they investigate his backstory, and proceed to mock, threaten, and torture anybody who refuses to talk. Siegel employs his trademark kineticism as director, but the real highlight is Gene L. Coon's treatment of Ernest Hemingway's original short story, which emphasizes the banal amid the brutal. Charlie and Lee may kill people, but their preoccupation with exercise and clean clothes gives their cavalier cruelty an appeal akin to the James Bond films of the period.

Lee Marvin was hungover when he filmed the last scene in *The Killers*, which perfectly suited his character's weakened state.

BRANDED TO KILL (1967)

Hollywood may have been in transition during the 1960s, but Japan's Nikkatsu Corporation was thriving, having established a winning formula with *mukokuseki akushun*, or "borderless action" films that filtered American noir and French New Wave through the prism of Japanese culture. *A Colt Is My Passport* (1967) is a prime example of a hit man story being given the Nikkatsu treatment, but *Branded to Kill*, released five months later and also starring Jô Shishido, represents the studio's peak. The film charts the mental decline of "Number Three Killer" (Shishido) after he botches an assignment and incurs the wrath of the mysterious "Number One Killer" (Kôji Nanbara). The plot, however, is secondary to director Seijun Suzuki's artistic impulses, as he ignores the script and impro-

Jô Shishido based the unnatural body language of his *Branded to Kill* character on the paintings of Edgar Degas.

vises absurdist touches like Number Three's rice-sniffing fetish or the death of a man via drainpipe. The blending of Pop art with satire is inspired, as evidenced by the use of animated masking in some scenes—a spoof of Japanese censorship. *Branded to Kill* was excoriated by critics upon its release, and Suzuki's rebelliousness led to his being temporarily blacklisted by the studio—but the film has endured as a totem of unadulterated creativity.

LE SAMOURAÏ (1967)

Branded to Kill brims with chaotic energy. If it was plugged into a heart-rate monitor, the film's pulse would rise and fall like a mountain range. *Le Samouraï*, by the same measure, would have a pulse like a flat, paved road. It's a masterclass in stillness, in letting the pictorial formalism of the medium dictate the pace, rather than character or plot. Director Jean-Pierre Melville understood the appeal of the noir tropes he assembled—the hit man, the enigmatic woman, the obsessed cop—but the writer-director avoided fleshing them out, as if to test the durability of their construction. Jef Costello (Alain Delon) may be a dead ringer for Philip Raven (*This Gun for Hire*), but gone are the monologues and any glimpses into the hit man's troubled past. Every-

Alain Delon described *Le Samouraï* as a study in "solitude." His character is silent during the film's opening ten minutes.

thing we learn about Costello comes from minute details, like the bottles of Evian water on his dresser or the ritualistic slide of his fingers across the brim of his fedora. An epigram of the samurai's Bushido code in the opening credits is the closest the film gets to explicit insight, and tellingly, the quote is fabricated by Melville. *Le Samouraï* crystallized the notion that less is more when it comes to hit man stories, a notion that proved to be immensely influential.

THE AMERICAN SOLDIER (1970)

Rainer Werner Fassbinder was so enamored with *Le Samouraï* that he was compelled to make his own version. The director's debut, *Love Is Colder Than Death* (1969), borrowed characters and poster designs, but it was his third film, *The American Soldier*, that blended Melville's influence with the idiosyncrasies that would eventually make Fassbinder one of the leading figures in the New German Cinema movement. The soldier in question is Ricky (Karl Scheydt), who upon returning from Vietnam agrees to wipe out Munich's criminal underworld. The film teeters on the edge of pastiche with its black-and-white cinematography and overwrought dialogue, but Fassbinder avoids it thanks to his atypical blend of existential dread and dry wit. Ricky's passionless romance with a policeman's girlfriend is offset by the bizarre possibility that his brother may be in love with him. Ricky's death echoes Costello's in *Le Samouraï*, but the scene goes on for so long, and the surviving characters are so overwhelmingly bereft that the tragedy turns to comedy. *The American Soldier* is a narrative composed of relentless left turns, each more entertaining and unexpected than the last.

THE MECHANIC (1972)

The Mechanic was originally conceived as a study in sexual manipulation. The hit men who drive

the plot, Arthur Bishop (Charles Bronson) and Steve McKenna (Jan-Michael Vincent), were supposed to be lovers who turn against each other when it's revealed that Bishop is being targeted by the "organization." United Artists wasn't having any of that. The studio forced screenwriter Lewis John Carlino to give Bishop a relationship with a call girl (another type of for-hire professional) and *The Mechanic* ended up as a straightforward thriller. Closer inspection, however, reveals a more complicated final product. The homoerotic text Carlino envisioned becomes subtext, and the killers' May-December romance turns into a father-son dynamic that only serves to heighten their twisted power struggle. There are plenty of memorable action scenes (and a killer ending) courtesy of director Michael Winner, but the film is at its best when it retreats to Bishop's den and explores the unspoken tension between the partners. The remnants of the romance that could have been, coupled with Bronson's uncharacteristically soulful performance, separates *The Mechanic* from the rest of the hit man films Hollywood released during the 1970s.

THE HIT (1984)

Hit men often kill from a distance. It's easier to execute a job when the target is dehumanized and viewed as an abstract concept devoid of feeling or thought. *The Hit* puts a fascinating spin on this practice. Orders from their powerful employer forces hit man partners Myron (Tim Roth) and Mitchell Braddock (John Hurt) to ferry their target from Spain to Paris before doing away with him. The target in question, Willie Parker (Terence Stamp), decides to embrace his fate with a Zen-like calm, which fascinates the youthful Myron and frustrates the increasingly disillusioned Braddock. The film's aesthetic is unlike any other in the hit man canon—earth tones and scenic backdrops set to flamenco music—but it's the sustained threat of violence that gives the film its gravitas. Everybody wants to kill everyone else at various points during the tense road trip. Stephen Frears shows nimble command in his second directorial effort, teasing out the complicated feelings each criminal has toward death while noting the irony

that none of them is actually ready when the time comes. A seminal "Brit Pack" release, *The Hit* is an unjustly overlooked early entry in the British neo-noir renaissance, paving the way for the trauma-fueled storytelling of filmmakers like Edgar Wright and Christopher Nolan.

Jean Reno and Natalie Portman as "cleaner" and pupil in *Léon: The Professional*.

LÉON: THE PROFESSIONAL (1994)

The 1980s had no shortage of hit man films, but most of their noir bona fides were downplayed in favor of commercial appeal. *Prizzi's Honor* (1985) and *Best Seller* (1987) were marketed on star power, which is what made the indie boom of the 1990s a welcome change of pace. Once more, the character's psychology dictated the storytelling. *Léon: The Professional* is about a hit man (Jean Reno) who assumes guardianship of an orphaned girl named Mathilda (Natalie Portman). Rather than finding her a proper home, Léon decides to train Mathilda so that she can take revenge against the corrupt DEA agents who murdered her family. The relationship between these two characters defies easy categorization, as Mathilda shows flashes of maturity that the stunted Léon struggles to comprehend (Reno revealed that he played the hit man as though he were "a little mentally slow.") They compensate for each other's weaknesses, which is a dynamic writer-director Luc Besson explores to unexpectedly tender effect. In watching Léon coach Mathilda through her first assignment, one can't help but develop a soft spot for these vengeful killers.

PULP FICTION (1994)

The impact of *Pulp Fiction* on popular culture cannot be overstated. Quentin Tarantino's sophomore effort changed the face of independent cinema, earned seven Oscar nominations, and inspired a generation of writer-directors to make their own nonlinear noir films. It also solidified the concept of the postmodern hit man. Vincent Vega (John Travolta) and Jules Winnfield (Samuel L. Jackson) kill people at the behest of Marsellus Wallace (Ving Rhames), but they do so while gabbing away like the duo from the 1964 version of *The Killers*, striking poses like the duo from the 1946 version, and cruising around L.A. side streets like the killer and his escorts in *Murder by Contract*. Tarantino's ability to repurpose dialogue and integrate cinematic references into an original story is perhaps his single greatest attribute—but his most subtle and daring choice is basing an entire subplot around the hit men's off-hours. Vega's aplomb with conversing and dancing during the "Vincent Vega and Marsellus Wallace's Wife" segment makes his profession secondary to his personality, effectively breaking down a wall that hit man stories had spent decades upholding. Suddenly, a character's bloody hands were the third or fourth most interesting thing about him.

Pulp Fiction established Samuel L. Jackson (right) as an Oscar-caliber actor and reestablished John Travolta as a leading man.

FALLEN ANGELS (1995)

Tarantino was quick to wield the influence *Pulp Fiction* afforded him. He founded a distribution company called Rolling Thunder Pictures, which exposed Western audiences to international cult films and exciting new writer-directors like Wong Kar-wai. The Hong Kong auteur shared Tarantino's propensity for nonlinear storytelling and pop soundtracks, but *Fallen Angels* proved he was more interested in the loneliness those stylistic choices exposed. The film's plot concerns Wong Chi-ming (Leon Lai), a hit man caught between the desire to quit and the begrudging sense of duty he feels toward his amorous partner (Michelle Reis). The beats may be standard—the last job, the lover scorned—but the presentation is not, due to Wong's mastery of framing and manipulation of frame rate. Stretches of *Fallen Angels* play like dreamy music videos, especially when cinematographer Christopher Doyle breaks out the wide-angle lenses. That said, the decision to kill the hit man fifteen minutes before the end credits remains the film's boldest move. By shifting focus to other characters, Wong suggests that loss, however devastating, can lead to unexpected forms of deliverance.

GHOST DOG: THE WAY OF THE SAMURAI (1999)

Jim Jarmusch's favorite hit man films are *Branded to Kill* and *Le Samouraï*, so it should come as no surprise that his own contribution to the canon, *Ghost Dog: The Way of the Samurai*, displays the influence of both on its sleeve. The title character (Forest Whitaker) having a bird land on his rifle scope is a direct callback to *Branded to Kill*, while his car-theft skills and white gloves recall *Le Samouraï*. These references add propulsion to what is otherwise a classic Jarmusch character study. When he's not committing heinous acts of violence, Ghost Dog aspires to kindness, as evidenced by his maintaining a rooftop pigeon coop and mentoring a local teenager. The character's adoption of the Bushido code isn't an honest reflection of his

Forest Whitaker was the only choice to play the titular hitman in *Ghost Dog: The Way of the Samurai*.

values so much as an attempt to reckon with his contradictory lifestyle; the inability to grow beyond this self-imposed system ultimately seals his fate. *Ghost Dog: The Way of the Samurai* has empathy for its hit man, but Jarmusch's willingness to interrogate the titular "way" is what makes it so gripping.

COLLATERAL (2004)

Michael Mann is a filmmaker who likes telling stories about exacting men. The efficiency with which crimes are executed (see: *Heat* [1995]) is often given as much focus as the justification for said crimes. It should then come as no surprise that Vincent (Tom Cruise), the focus of Mann's neo-noir masterpiece *Collateral*, is among the deadliest hit men ever depicted. Vincent

Tom Cruise's tactical draw proved so deadly that scenes from *Collateral* are used during handgun training lessons.

wields a pistol as though it were an extension of his hand, but it's his cunning, his ability to coerce and manipulate, that terrifies his cabbie hostage, Max (Jamie Foxx). The two men lay waste to Los Angeles over the course of a single day, and yet their mutual contempt for each other leads to moments of genuine insight. The hit man and the cabbie who spend their lives being invisible to the rest of the world see right through each other's facades, and it results in some of the finest exchanges of both Cruise's and Foxx's careers. *Collateral* is too interested in human behavior to depict these men as being all good or all bad. It's a film that's comfortable with the truth being somewhere in between, like the spotless divider in Max's dented car.

IN BRUGES (2008)

There are incompetent hit men, and then there's Ray (Colin Farrell). The dense Irishman killed a child during a seemingly routine assignment and he's been sent to Belgium with his mentor, Ken (Brendan Gleeson), to await further instructions. Ken is secretly ordered to shoot Ray, but he's so taken aback by the latter's suicide attempt that he puts his gun away and talks Ray down. These are the farcical happenings that fuel *In Bruges*. Playwright Martin McDonagh threads the needle between sadness and slapstick nonsense in his directorial debut, while convincing the viewer to root for characters who would be reprehensible were they not so funny. The insults they hurl at one another are as colorful as they are quotable, but it's the situational writing in McDonagh's screenplay that sets the film apart. The motivations of each character are so well established that when the final act devolves into a mélange of dumb luck and gruesome destruction, the viewer is conflicted about who to root for. *In Bruges* subverts the romantic ideal of the hit man more than any other film on this list.

KILLING THEM SOFTLY (2012)

Hit man films took many forms in the 2010s. *The Iceman* (2012) and *The Irishman* (2019) upend the notion of the lone-wolf killer by depicting their real-life protagonists as family men, while *The American* (2010) and *The Gunman* (2015) mine the style of French crime novelist Jean-Patrick Manchette for measured suspense and mindless action, respectively. Then there's *Killing Them Softly*, which posits the hit man as a side effect of a broken system. An adaptation of George V. Higgins's novel *Cogan's Trade* (1974), the film details the aftermath of a robbery that takes place during a Mafia poker game. The men who commit the robbery, Frankie (Scoot McNairy) and Russell (Ben Mendelsohn), know they're doomed, and the hit man tasked with hunting them down, Jackie Cogan (Brad Pitt), displays none of the patience or charm of his predecessors. He wants money and will put a bullet in anybody's head in order to collect, plain and simple. *Killing Them Softly* makes no bones about the brutality of criminal life, but Andrew Dominik updates the time period of the novel to incorporate the 2008 financial crisis and presidential election. The modern backdrop allows the writer-director to extend his nihilist outlook to American life writ large. Is it subtle? Not really. It is, however, extremely effective.

Brad Pitt was instrumental in getting *Killing Them Softly* made. He produced the film in addition to playing hitman Jackie Cogan.

THE KILLER (2023)

The twenty-first century has reimagined the hit man through conflicted, comedic, and political lenses. *The Killer* resets the template. The film is based on the French graphic novel of the same name, but the source material is merely an impetus for screenwriter Andrew Kevin Walker and director David Fincher to see how much they can strip away while maintaining the basic shape of a hit man story. The eponymous killer (Michael Fassbender) has neither a name or a past. What he does have is a hat and coat reminiscent of Philip Raven and Jef Costello, as well as a disciplined routine that makes them look improvisational by comparison. Fincher's decision to frame the hit man's quest as a procedural makes perfect sense given his exacting nature, but it's executed with such masterful simplicity that it seems revelatory. The foundation laid by Walker and Fincher allows every technical flourish, narrative twist, and The Smiths needle-drop to hit with ten times the expected impact. *The Killer* doesn't break the mold so much as present viewers with the sleekest model to date—it pays tribute to the cinematic history of the hit man while affirming his place within the medium's legacy. ∎

Michael Fassbender bides his time in *The Killer*. The actor came out of a four-year hiatus to play the title character.

CRUEL YULE

Noir and the Holiday Season

Jeremy Arnold

*a*s film noir emerged in the early 1940s and proliferated into the 1950s, so did Christmas movies. The end of the Second World War in particular spurred both film modes into overdrive across Hollywood. Yet, with a single exception, the conventions of Christmas movies and film noir never completely joined to create a bona fide "Christmas noir."

This may raise eyebrows among those who can instantly reel off any number of noirs with Christmas *in* them, from *Christmas Holiday* (1944) to *Beware, My Lovely* (1952). But as with most debates over Christmas movies—and heated arguments over "noir or not?"—the core dispute is really over definition. Neither film noir nor Christmas movies were recognized genres in studio-era Hollywood. No director in 1944 ever said, "My next picture is a Christmas movie" (or "holiday movie") or "I'm shooting a film noir next week." The labels would come later, with hindsight. Noir is a visual style, a storytelling attitude, a cinematic movement. But "Christmas movie"? That slippery and relatively modern term remains open to personal definition because it has not historically constituted a distinct genre *or* style. It validly means whatever a person decides it to mean, from, say, any escapist movie that one enjoys revisiting at Christmastime to all movies containing even a glimpse of the holiday.

In the course of screening films for my book *Christmas in the Movies*, I settled on my own definition: a movie in which some aspect of the holiday season plays a meaningful role in the storytelling. Meaningful, that is, to the characters' journeys, the story's emotional concerns, and the audience's takeaway. Since the season can mean different things at different points in our lives, from compassion, togetherness, or nostalgia to loneliness, cynicism, or exasperation, a variety of story types can become fodder for Christmas movies. A common thread, however, is how the season works as an active force on-screen, often serving as a catalyst for characters to heal or unite.

As a result, holiday movies tend to stress—and end on—notes of optimism and positive transformation, usually through cheerful comedy or heartwarming drama. This is the antithesis of film noir,

Gene Kelly (right), Deanna Durbin, and Richard Whorf in *Christmas Holiday*, which despite its title barely acknowledges Christmas.

which stresses fatalism, cynicism, and sinister undercurrents of society that draw characters into a sordid world from which there is usually no escape. Christmas movies guide characters up, toward their better, positive natures; noir pulls them down, toward the depths of their own destructive impulses.

The social upheaval brought by World War II pushed noir and Christmas movies even further into these diametrically opposed patterns. Over the first half of the decade, families were torn apart as millions of Americans went off to war. During the second half, families attempted to rebuild themselves, with or without the return of their loved ones. Families were fracturing *and* reuniting on an enormous scale, and Christmas became a more frequent narrative device in movies generally, often representing the family unit. Film noir, on the other hand, tapped into the pessimistic currents of the postwar era, especially the alienation and hopelessness that some veterans experienced as they struggled to fit back into a changed society.

Occasionally a Christmas movie incorporated noir motifs as counterpoint: *It's a Wonderful Life* (1946) depicts George Bailey's time in Pottersville as a film noir nightmare, and even *I'll Be Seeing You* (1944), a romantic drama, borrows a bit of noir style for its sequences of Joseph Cotten's character suffering from PTSD. More commonly it was the other way around, with Christmas popping up in noirs as an ironic contrast to sinister tales. While that wasn't enough to make them Christmas movies (though some came close), it has nonetheless made them entertaining to watch during the holiday season. One of the earliest examples is the aforementioned *Christmas Holiday*, starring Gene Kelly and Deanna Durbin—enough to make anyone expect a bright Yuletide musical. In fact, it is hard-edged noir from one of the movement's great directors, Robert Siodmak, and Christmas is just a backdrop, barely even mentioned. Early on, when a character says, "Christmas is only for kids; it's not for us," it's as if the movie itself is saying, "Christmas has no place in this kind of film."

More noirs with holiday settings followed. *The Suspect* (1944), superbly directed once again by

Charles Laughton contemplates murder as he gazes at his venomous wife, played by Rosalind Ivan, on Christmas Eve in *The Suspect*.

Not even a Christmas tree can lighten the dynamic between Joan Leslie and Louis Hayward in *Repeat Performance*.

Siodmak, has a sympathetic Charles Laughton killing his shrewish wife on Christmas Eve and trying to get away with it, with the audience rooting for him all the way. *Lady on a Train* (1945), a diverting noir-musical-comedy hybrid, uses the holiday as fodder for humor and lightness, and stops in its tracks for an exquisite rendition of "Silent Night" by Deanna Durbin on a snowy Christmas Eve. *Lady in the Lake* (1946), a Raymond Chandler adaptation, opens with a medley of Christmas carols over Yuletide-themed title cards, but again the holiday is no more than a setting. The fantasy noir *Repeat Performance* (1947), in which Joan Leslie relives an entire calendar year after shooting her husband, includes a brief but affecting Christmas Eve scene in which Leslie trims a tree while reminiscing nostalgically to an unresponsive Louis Hayward.

Kiss of Death (1947) uses the season right away to draw sympathy for Victor Mature's character, Nick Bianco, as he robs a jeweler on Christmas Eve: "This is how Nick went Christmas shopping for his kid," a narrator intones. The stylish B noir *I Wouldn't Be in Your Shoes* (1948) has a character sentenced to be executed just after the holiday for a crime he didn't commit. Christmas feels strikingly ominous and lonely when it enters the story halfway through, with a detective working through the night into Christmas morning to try and unmask the real killer. "It's Christmas Eve and I'm lonesome and afraid," says one character.

The holiday plays a briefer role in *They Live by Night* (1949), providing a moment of respite for the doomed young lovers on the run, and a more consistent role in *The Reckless Moment* (1949), underscoring the notion of a fractured family that is vital to the tense story. *Backfire* (1950) culminates with Dane Clark recounting his murder of another character on Christmas Eve—ironically as carolers sing "Deck the Halls" in the background.

In *Roadblock* (1951), Christmas nudges perennial tough guy Charles McGraw to perhaps his most romantic screen moment. After decorating a Christmas tree, he pulls Joan Dixon into his arms and says poignantly, "I want you so bad I can't think straight. You're what I want for Christmas, the day after, the Fourth of July, Saturday nights, all the days there are." Dixon's classic response drains the Christmas warmth from the room in a flash: "And I want you, Joe . . . but not as an insurance cop making $350 a month!" *Beware, My Lovely* frequently displays its seasonal setting via wreaths, trees, and ornaments in the frame, as counterpoint to a taut tale of unstable handyman Robert Ryan terrorizing Ida Lupino.

The 3-D noir *I, the Jury* (1953) is also laden with holiday references—shots of Christmas cards to establish new scenes, Christmas music throughout, and even Elisha Cook Jr. winding up dead in a Santa costume—but they don't bring real meaning to the proceedings. The spellbinding *The Night of the Hunter* (1955), on the other hand, brings Christmas in at the very end to emphasize the metaphorical rebirth of the children who have been terrorized throughout by Robert Mitchum. It helps foster a cathartic release from the darkness for these traumatized child characters (not to mention for the audience). In later decades, Christmas would feature in such neo-noir pictures as *The Silent Partner* (1978), *Reindeer Games* (2000), and *The Ice Harvest* (2005), but here, too, the holiday remains mostly a setting.

Two classic gems make for fascinating test cases of whether noir and Christmas can truly combine. Christmas in a sense prevents the first, *Cover Up* (1949), from *becoming* a film noir. Directed by Alfred E. Green, the picture skirts the edges of the noir style with its tale of an insurance investigator, Dennis O'Keefe, working to unravel a murder mystery in a small town and finding the residents unwilling to talk; they and sheriff William Bendix all seem to be covering up the killer's identity. The story takes place over the days leading up to Christmas, with the season a constant presence.

In its first three minutes following the main titles, the film establishes an intriguing tension between light Christmastime romance and ominous mystery. O'Keefe and Barbara Britton arrive by train at a small-town station, engage in a charming meet-cute involving a bundle of Christmas presents, continue their blossoming romance during a bus ride to town, and arrive to Britton's family waiting at the bus stop, which prompts a cheerful welcome. There's even a sidewalk Santa, bell in hand. But at two points during this jaunty sequence, the upbeat tone and score are interrupted by startling flashes

After great trauma, a welcome moment of joy and relief—linked to Christmas—for Billy Chapin and Lillian Gish in *The Night of the Hunter.*

The trappings of the season provide tonal counterpoint to the increasingly tense dynamic between Robert Ryan and Ida Lupino in *Beware, My Lovely*.

Christmas helps nudge Dennis O'Keefe and Barbara Britton together in *Cover Up*.

of menace: there is news of a mysterious, supposed suicide, and O'Keefe seems to know something about it.

That tonal seesaw between lightness and mystery, joy and peril, grounds the audience in a story pattern that will continue all the way to the film's denouement, late at night on Christmas Eve. The effect is of a push and pull between Christmas movie and film noir. It's as if each is vying with the other to dominate the story, the characters, and the imagery, with the light holiday scenes pushing the dark scenes out of the frame, only for the darker mode to push right back. *Cover Up* "wants" to be a film noir, but Christmas wins the battle. In fact, the holiday winds up being the key to *Cover Up*'s solution and ultimate meaning, though this only becomes apparent after a last-minute story revelation—which makes the audience realize in retrospect that this has been a genuine Christmas movie all along.

The season keeps *Cover Up* mostly lighthearted, driving leisurely scenes of family gatherings, comic charm, and an aura of gentleness, all of which keep the sinister moments in check. One sequence that captures this dynamic well has Britton's father (Art Baker) trying to retrieve an incriminating gun that he had hidden in a piece of furniture, only to discover that the gun is not there. The camera lingers on Baker as he figures out what the audience already knows—that his daughter removed the weapon in an effort to protect him from harm and suspicion. This realization profoundly moves him (Baker plays it beautifully) and spurs him to find Britton and express his love for her with a tender bit of dialogue. A hidden gun, suspicion, and incrimination are perfect ingredients for noir, but this sequence takes them in a completely different direction, to a pure Christmas-movie payoff: a family drawn closer together in loving connection.

Cover Up is a model illustration of why Christmas and film noir don't workably mix. The stronger the Christmas movie element—the transformation to a kinder self, the overcoming of family dysfunction, the blossoming of love—the further from noir a film travels, since those elements are not germane

As Lori, Molly McCarthy in *Blast of Silence* is repeatedly linked to an optimistic view of Christmastime, but she's no match for the dominating force of noir.

to noir. Perhaps the sole exception to this pattern lies in a film that doesn't try to incorporate the positive aspects of Christmastime but rather the darker ones, such as alienation and cynicism. They fit seamlessly into *Blast of Silence* (1961), a superbly compelling noir that explores the mind of a weary assassin as he prepares to carry out a hit in New York after Christmas Day.

Suspenseful and raw, *Blast of Silence* was made for $65,000 by independent first-time filmmakers Allen Baron (who wrote, directed, and plays the assassin) and Merrill Brody (who produced, photographed, and coedited). In twenty-two shooting days across four months, they filmed with handheld equipment on locations all over the city—from St. Mark's Place and the original Penn Station to Rockefeller Plaza, Staten Island, and Harlem—making this a fascinating and moody time capsule of New York City circa 1960.

The grittiness of the filmmaking aligns with the tone of the story, established right away by nihilistic narration read in the second person by the gravelly voiced actor Lionel Stander—uncredited because he was blacklisted at the time. (The narration was written by blacklisted screenwriter Waldo Salt under a pseudonym.) "You were born with hate," Stander rasps as Frankie Bono, the assassin, enters the city. "Christmas gives you the creeps." The voice-over positively seethes with contempt for the city, its people, the world at large, and Christmas.

The holiday serves a far stronger purpose in *Blast of Silence* than mere ironic counterpoint. Its frequent mentions in the voice-over and visuals effectively force the audience to watch this entire tale through the prism of Christmastime. Moreover, "hatred" of the holiday is something that audiences will have likely experienced in their lives—perhaps not to Bono's extremes, but to a degree. Who has not occasionally grown fed up with the holiday season, resenting its manufactured joy, its commercialism, or its overly saccharine nature? *Blast of Silence* takes this attitude and runs with it, using it to build and drive the character of Bono himself. Persistent scornful references to the holiday bring the audience into his cynical, bitter mindset, through which he sees the tropes of Christmas as phony and insufferable. When the story reaches Christmas morning and the narration declares, "December twenty-fifth . . . You have all of Christmas Day to kill," the moment feels perfect for this picture.

There is zero sentiment in *Blast of Silence*, no transformation or happy ending. When Bono does reveal a flicker of desire to transform, and the plot offers the slightest possibility for love to enter his life—two Christmas-movie tropes—the film violently swats both notions away and pulls Bono even more firmly into its noir grasp. Unlike in *Cover Up*, the buoyant version of Christmas here loses the battle, and *Blast of Silence* stays completely true to itself with one of the bleakest, most pessimistic endings in film noir. The script even includes a reference to Christmas right before the final fade-out—illustrating just how embedded the season is in the storytelling. ■

Adapted from portions of the author's Christmas in the Movies—Revised and Expanded Edition, *published by Running Press and Turner Classic Movies.*

PROFILES
SECTION TWO

UNHINGED

TIMOTHY CAREY'S WILD RIDE THROUGH NOIR AND BEYOND

By Steve Kronenberg

"I always thought if you really want to be a good actor, you've got to be able to fart in public." That salute to the toot was uttered by Timothy Carey. Watching him slide, slog, and sleaze his way through a variety of dark and deranged performances is always . . . a gas. His unpredictability, brazenness, and sheer chutzpah were perfectly suited to a life in noir—both on and off screen.

Timothy Agoglia Carey was born and raised in Brooklyn. At age fifteen, he lied his way into the Marines by using his older brother's birth certificate before being booted out when the corps discovered his real age. Membership in a weight-lifting club gave him the hulking physique he'd use for movie roles as henchmen and thugs. He coupled his intimidating bulk with a mug made for menace. "My head is too fucking large," he once said. "My eyes . . . Jesus, I look sleepy all the time . . . my mouth hangs open most of the time. Gives me the look of an idiot or a criminal. Or an idiot criminal." He saw a future in Hollywood and thumbed his way West.

King Leer: Carey gets toothsome with Gene Nelson, as fellow cast members Phyllis Kirk, James Bell, Charles Bronson, and Ted de Corsia seem bemused in *Crime Wave*.

After being kicked off the Columbia Pictures lot during an impromptu visit, Carey hitched to New Mexico where Billy Wilder was filming *Ace in the Hole* (1951). He made his film debut by cajoling one of Wilder's assistants into tossing him a bit part, but he was quickly fired when he tried to muscle in on a scene alongside Kirk Douglas. It was the first of many confrontations Carey would have with directors and actors. "It didn't take me long to find out that the more enthusiastic I got about my work," he said, "the less enthusiastic some of my fellow players got about me." He angered Marlon Brando by spilling beer on him during an improvised scene in *The Wild One* (1953). Two years later, he was nearly assaulted by Elia Kazan, who despised his guttural dialogue delivery as the bordello bouncer who manhandles James Dean in *East of Eden* (1955). Carey's talent outweighed his volatility, and filmmakers matched him with roles that suited his eccentric approach. Every crime film in which he appeared is worth savoring, from *Revolt in the Big House* (1958) to *The Outfit* (1973), but his place in noir was fixed with a handful of bizarre and imaginative portrayals.

It was in *Crime Wave* (1954), as sadistic hood Johnny Haslett, that Carey developed the rictus grin and teeth-gritting grimace that would define his uniquely demented persona. While cohorts Ted de Corsia and Charles Buchinsky (Bronson) pull a bank heist, Carey gleefully torments hostage Phyllis Kirk. After filming, he apologized to Kirk for playing it too creepy. "I affected a twitch like a narcotics addict," he recalled. "I turned on a low, sensual, half-crazy laugh, gritted my teeth and dug my hands into her shoulders."

Carey lauded Stanley Kubrick for his ability to tell stories from "the perspective of criminals and psychopaths." Kubrick returned the compliment by casting Carey as reptilian sharpshooter Nikki Arcane in *The Killing* (1956). In order to divert cops and crowds from the racetrack robbery he's planning, Johnny Clay (Sterling Hayden) hires Arcane to shoot a horse favored to win an important race. Carey plays Arcane as a mass of tics and twitches. He cuddles a puppy while aiming a shotgun at his intended target, fidgets and foams, licks his lips, wipes his eyes, stutters and spits racist slurs at the track's security guard (James Edwards). Arcane is the only member of Clay's cadre who's certifiably psychotic. The film's costar Marie Windsor vividly remembered Carey: "Timothy Carey—he is

Carey recalled that after this sadistic scene in *Crime Wave*, costar Phyllis Kirk "broke and got hysterical."

Sterling Hayden and Carey mull over their contract and prepare for target practice in *The Killing*.

really weird. When I won the *Look* [magazine] award for best supporting, Kubrick wanted to shoot publicity shots with Carey's house in the background. You can't believe this guy. He slept on a torn mattress with no sheets, windows that had burlap hanging instead of curtains. It looked worse than Skid Row, but Kubrick really thought he had charisma."

Bayou (1957), rereleased in 1961 as *Poor White Trash*, is more pulp than noir, but Carey provides the transcendence. In his first genuinely kinetic performance, he plays a lecherous swamp rat pursuing a nubile teenager (Lita Milan). He's a frenzied gumbo of grit, grime, and gris-gris, perpetually on the move, thrusting his hips and convulsing in a spontaneous and spasmodic dance inspired by famed burlesque performer "Cat Girl" Lilly Christine.

"If you wanna be a good actor," Carey mused, "go to the zoo and watch the rhino—look at the way he moves. Watch the weasel, every part involves a new body pattern." Carey applied that aberrant approach to his role as the doomed Private Maurice Ferol in *Paths of Glory* (1957), his renowned reunion with Kubrick. The film doesn't qualify as noir, but it's a showcase for Carey's versatility and ingenuity, allowing him to deliver his most nuanced and sympathetic performance. Carey plays Ferol as guileless, almost childlike, refusing to accept his death sentence for a trumped-up charge of treason under fire. He literally steals the movie's climax, breaking from the script and breaking down as he's led to a firing squad. Kubrick approved Carey's ad lib, but it aroused the ire of Emile Meyer, who plays the priest accompanying him to his execution. "Emile Meyer wanted to slap me," Carey recalled, "and Adolphe Menjou didn't care much for me. I had a toy monkey and I was walking around with holes in my shoes."

Carey's triumph in *Paths of Glory* was somewhat blunted by an outrageous offscreen incident.

The Eyes Have It: Carey delivered his most sympathetic performance as the guileless Pvt. Maurice Ferol in *Paths of Glory*.

Jealous over the publicity Kirk Douglas received during location shooting in Germany, Carey faked his own kidnapping by convincing a couple in Munich to tie him up and leave him bound and gagged on a roadside. After refusing to cooperate with police, he finally confessed to the stunt. Both Kubrick and producer James B. Harris angrily banned him from the set and replaced him with a double during the film's battle scenes. "I will never work with him again," declared Kubrick. "He was almost dangerous to have around . . . brilliant, but impossible."

Deploring Hollywood's "rotten money culture," Carey formed Frenzy Productions to independently produce and release his own movies. The studio's debut feature was *The World's Greatest Sinner* (1962), which he wrote, produced, directed, and financed over the course of four years. The film mirrors Carey's own persona: ragged, incoherent, undisciplined, audacious. He cast himself in the title role as Clarence Hilliard, a bored insurance salesman who trades mediocrity for megastardom and megalomania. Inspired by the manic crowds at a rockabilly concert, Hilliard begins his quest for power by grabbing a guitar, donning a shiny suit, and hitting the road as a rock musician. Renaming himself "God Hilliard," he channels Elvis Presley, James Brown, and Jerry Lee Lewis, whipping audiences into a frenzy. Dissatisfied with mere show biz glitz, Hilliard forms the Eternal Man's Party, runs for president, and develops a rabid cult following. Sporting a sick grimace, he seduces wealthy widows and underage girls, incites riots, encourages acolytes to commit suicide. As his sanity unravels, Hilliard fancies himself a deity. He's finally brought low when he challenges the Christian God to appear before him. The Almighty answers the call, stalking and overcoming Hilliard with a snail trail of blood and slime.

Carey labeled Hilliard "an Elvis Presley who becomes a Billy Graham who becomes a Father Divine." It's a tidy but taut description. His screenplay is remarkably prescient, portending such power-crazed cult leaders as Jim Jones, David Koresh, and Charles Manson. Early in the film, Hilliard impulsively smashes a guitar, anticipating the pyrotechnics of Jimi Hendrix and The Who. Whether in bed or on stage, Carey elaborates on his *Bayou* hoodoo by getting naked, dancing with snakes, and writhing and screaming in a rock-inspired St. Vitus' Dance. When the film closes with Hilliard a beaten pseudo-god, Carey wins our sympathy; his body crumples to a heap, his sad eyes turn skyward, his face frowns

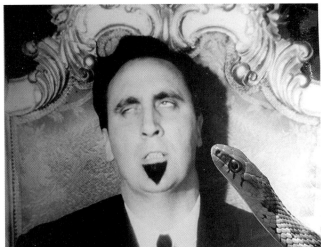

Snake oil salesman Clarence Hilliard meets his match in this cold-blooded scene from *The World's Greatest Sinner*.

and furrows. During filming, he melded Method with madness. "Tim *became* God Hilliard," recalled supporting actor Gil Barreto. "We really had a God in person on the set. It was very difficult to be with Tim at times."

The World's Greatest Sinner's grungy texture bears the taint of low-budget noir. The movie opens on a black screen, with unreliable narration from a Satanic boa constrictor voiced by actor Paul Frees. Carey enlisted Poverty Row maestros Edgar G. Ulmer (billed as Ove H. Sehasted) and Ray Dennis Steckler to assist in principal photography, which accounts for the film's surreal camerawork. Shifts in tone and lighting mark Hilliard's gradual descent into depravity. Some scenes are lit so dimly that faces and bodies become indiscernible. High-key lighting is used to depict Hilliard in distorted close-ups congregating with his disciples. Walls are pocked with shadows that mysteriously fade from sight. The entire film has the look of an unedited rough cut: scenes are filmed sideways and upside down, jump cuts abruptly skew continuity, and the screen periodically goes dark. The film is more spit than polish, but its crudity and nihilism parallel Hilliard's psychic dissolution. With its iconoclastic style, it also serves as an act of rebellion, a kiss off to the Hollywood Carey loathed.

Carey stayed true to the film's rock 'n' roll vibe by tapping a young Frank Zappa to compose the score, a jumble of rockabilly, classical, and jazz notes. Zappa conducted the Pomona Valley Symphony Orchestra, recorded the soundtrack in a local theater, and mixed it inside a rented truck. Carey gave Zappa his first important gig; Zappa showed his gratitude by trashing the film as "the world's worst movie."

The World's Greatest Sinner premiered on January 30, 1963, at Hollywood's Vista Continental Theatre. Before the film unspooled Carey took the stage, pulled out a .38, and fired three shots over the audience. Shock turned to awe and puzzlement when the reels began rolling. Over the years, reaction to the film has been mixed. "The press said I was the world's greatest ham," Carey recalled, "and that *The World's Greatest Sinner* was a travesty of the arts." The *Los Angeles Times* denounced the movie and condemned the theater for exhibiting it. Others would disagree. Elvis Presley begged Carey for a copy of the film. Martin Scorsese cited it as "one of the three great rock 'n' roll films." *Village Voice* critic J. Hoberman commended it as "the missing link between *A Face in the Crowd* [1957] and *Wild in the Streets* [1968]." John Cassavetes likened it to the work of Sergei Eisenstein. Comparisons to *Citizen Kane* (1941) may not be as pointless as they seem. Both films are fiercely individual visions of the will to power and its corrupting influence. Carey's film arguably ventures even further, predicting America's fixation on religious leaders, politicians, celebrities, and social media gurus. The May 1,

1962, issue of *Daily Variety* published a letter Carey directed to Nikita Khrushchev, offering to send the Soviet premier a copy of the movie and claiming it "can help the world, especially people out to conquer it." He never received a reply.

"John Cassavetes was different!" Carey exclaimed. "He would inspire people . . . he was always there to lend a helping hand." After Cassavetes effusively praised *The World's Greatest Sinner*, he and Carey became kindred souls. Both men were mavericks indifferent to the strictures of the Hollywood establishment. Like Kubrick, Cassavetes saw Carey's softer side and cast him as sensitive street-corner poet Morgan Morgan in *Minnie and Moskowitz* (1971). A more pensive Carey emerged when Cassavetes chose him to play Flo, the cerebral hit man in *The Killing of a Chinese Bookie* (1976). Assigned to take out club owner Cosmo Vittelli (Ben Gazzara), Flo cleverly deceives both his bosses and the audience. Carey imbues the character with mood swings, treading between affability and malice. Throughout the film, he's stoic and serene, delivering one of his most disarming performances. Flo is a man of conscience and culture, presaging the contemplative hoods played by James Gandolfini in *True Romance* (1993) and *The Sopranos* (1999–2007). Watch the way he leans into Gazzara during intimate conversations, speaking barely above a whisper, reminiscing about his father and bemoaning society's ills. "That jerk Karl Marx said opium is the religion of the people," he muses. "He was wrong, it's money." Flo misquotes Marx, but we'll forgive that because he gets the message right anyway.

Despite his prodigious talent, Carey's volatility cost him several crucial roles: Luca Brasi in *The Godfather* (1972), by demanding too much money and too many perks; Bernie Moran in *The Conversation* (1974), when he ordered producer Fred Roos to come to his house and mow his lawn; Don Fanucci in *The Godfather Part II* (1974), when he was axed for pulling a gun on Francis Ford Coppola; and Joe Cabot in *Reservoir Dogs* (1992), after a nervous Harvey Keitel threatened to walk if forced to work with Carey, who was replaced by the equally volcanic Lawrence Tierney. (Quentin Tarantino dedicated the film to Carey, Tierney, and several other noir luminaries.)

Undaunted, Carey wrote and directed an unsold TV pilot entitled *Tweet's Ladies of Pasadena*, about a character who makes clothing for animals (he wanted to show the film to an audience, then send it through a shredder, spraying the attendees with bits of celluloid). Through the 1970s and 1980s, he occupied the small screen in everything from *Charlie's Angels* (1976–81) to *Columbo* (1971–78), as the rumpled detective's favorite chili chef. He remained indefatigable until a stroke claimed him on May 11, 1994, at age sixty-five.

Timothy Carey's outré legacy endures, embodied in outliers like Crispin Glover, Joaquin Phoenix, and the late Heath Ledger. It's comforting to think that somehow, somewhere, he's still marauding through movie screens, stealing scenes, and pissing off everyone around him. ■

WALTER MATTHAU
NOIR'S RUMPLED ICON

By Vince Keenan

The transformation took less than a year. *Charley Varrick* was released on October 19, 1973. *The Laughing Policeman* made a mordant Christmas gift two months later. By the time *The Taking of Pelham One Two Three* reached theaters on October 2, 1974, Walter Matthau, Tony- and Oscar-winning comedy star, had become the hangdog face of neo-noir.

This remarkable run of films was prompted, in part, by spite. "I've been playing different sorts of roles all my life," Matthau told the *New York Times* during *The Taking of Pelham One Two Three*'s production. "It's just that I fell into seven years of comedies and I began to resent the fact that's all I was sent." He starred in *Charley Varrick*, he explained to the *Los Angeles Times*, because his agent wanted "to establish a precedent that I can indeed do a straight picture . . . that would not lose money." (Losing money, as it happens, was a subject on which Matthau could speak with authority.)

Those three titles account for Matthau's reputation in noir, but he worked the dark side of the street from his first days onscreen. Also, a fourth film from that era warrants inclusion in the conversation, given its pitch-black premise and Matthau's pitiless performance. Trouble is, it's a comedy.

It's petty theft to say that Matthau steals *Slaughter on 10th Avenue* as union boss Al Dahlke, but a crime is a crime.

THE ITCH FOR SCRATCH

Matthau frequently said he "congealed" into being an actor. In 1974, he summarized his process for the *Pittsburgh Press*: "I use the Matthau Method which is, just say the lines and don't imitate anybody."

An unsung element of the Matthau Method is his longtime gambling habit, which affected the trajectory of his career. *Charley Varrick* actor Andrew Robinson recalled asking Matthau how he'd become a star. Matthau said the key was his bookie asking if he'd rather have his arms or legs broken; he took every job he was offered after that. His debts compelled Matthau to detour into syndicated television as his stock as a stage and screen actor was rising, top-lining the short-lived crime drama *Tallahassee 7000* (1961–62). Shortly after breaking through in Hollywood, Matthau needed to cash a check at a racetrack in order to place a bet. He yelled into the stands, "Where are my fans?" Offering to stand him the money: actor George Raft. Matthau asked him how he knew the check would be any good.

"I've seen your work," Raft replied. "I'll take a chance."

After achieving success on Broadway, Matthau made his film debut as a villain opposite Burt Lancaster in *The Kentuckian* (1955). He continued mining that vein in his early noir outings. The middling gangland drama *Slaughter on 10th Avenue* (1957) withers in the shadow of *On the Waterfront* (1954), never living up to its title or its use of Richard Rodgers's music. But Matthau brings freshness to the role of union kingpin Al Dahlke, tough enough to have worked his way up the ranks while possessing sufficient polish to be entrusted with authority. He relishes his position, cutting backroom deals in a Chinese restaurant while cheerily offering ribs made with "some kind of plum sauce," wheedling and bullying in the same genial tone of voice. It's petty theft to say Matthau steals the movie, but a crime is a crime. A memorable introduction sets up his New Orleans gangster Maxie Fields in *Elvis*

Presley's best movie and sole noir, *King Creole* (1958). Maxie threatens his mistress Ronnie (Carolyn Jones) when he spies her being friendly with Elvis's Danny Fisher. Ronnie says she's heard Danny sing, so Maxie forces him to perform in order to prove Ronnie isn't lying. Elvis then belts out "Trouble" while staring Matthau down, the first of several set-tos between their characters.

The rare actor who turned to directing solely because he needed the money, Matthau claimed that when he stepped behind the camera on *Gangster Story* (1959), "I made out the W-2 forms and held the boom." (Tellingly, the godawful opening credits song is entitled "The Itch for Scratch.") Running a mere sixty-eight minutes, the movie boasts looped dialogue throughout and choppy editing courtesy of adult film pioneer Radley Metzger. Matthau unfairly lambasted the screenplay, a tidy effort that prefigures *Charley Varrick*. Matthau's thief, Jack Martin, is ruthless—as the film opens, he's killed two cops while escaping custody—but cunning. Several bits of business lend him an outlaw charm, like his arranging a bogus film shoot (to which he invites actual policemen) as cover for a bank robbery. There's even a serviceable plot, with a crime boss offering to bankroll Martin's heists only to set him up when Martin falls for a woman and tries to walk away. An RKO version of this script would be hailed as a minor classic. Instead, *Gangster Story* is a curio thanks to its Ed Wood production values. Matthau would marry leading lady Carol Grace, but he'd never direct again.

After winning a Tony Award in 1962 for the farce *A Shot in the Dark* and racking up several more prestige supporting roles in film, Matthau returned to the noir wheelhouse. The plot of *Mirage* (1965) is baroque even by amnesia movie standards; what matters is gray-flannelled executive David Stillwell (Gregory Peck) loses his memory and finds mayhem. Matthau's Ted Caselle is the private eye hired by Stillwell at random to investigate his past; turns out he's an ex–refrigerator repairman who just hung out his shingle, and Stillwell is his first client. Caselle grounds the enterprise, never blanching at preposterous twists and making savvy deductions. "Wouldn't it be hilarious if you *did* know what you were doing?" Stillwell asks him. Peck later said his "main contribution to the film was that I hired Walter." During production, director Edward Dmytryk told Matthau that he would "become the greatest character actor in the business." Matthau scoffed in response: "I'm gonna be a leading man." A rare one-two punch pushed the performer to that seemingly unlikely pantheon.

Mirage opened in theaters while Matthau was the toast of Broadway thanks to *The Odd Couple* (1965). Matthau won his second Tony Award for Neil Simon's play, and immediately moved on to another triumph. Billy Wilder—who had toyed with casting the then-unknown actor in *The Seven Year Itch* (1955)—gave Matthau the plum role of ambulance chaser "Whiplash Willie" Gingrich, who coerces his brother-in-law (Jack Lemmon) into a fraudulent lawsuit, in *The Fortune Cookie* (1966). The film marked the initial pairing of two actors who would become an enduring big-screen duo and longtime friends. Matthau took home an Academy Award for Best Supporting Actor for his performance. The incorrigible gambler had bet on himself and come up flush: as he'd told Dmytryk, he was now a leading man. To cement that status, he would turn in part to a trio of crime dramas—and a comedy with a darker heart than any of them.

"DID I SAY SHE WAS PRIMITIVE? I RETRACT THAT. SHE'S FERAL."

A man marries a woman with the intent of murdering her. A classic noir setup. The difference is that Elaine May, who wrote and directed *A New Leaf* (1971) as well as starring as the prospective victim, played the premise for laughs.

Matthau's Henry Graham spends as only someone who came from wealth can. But those profligate practices have rendered him, in the words of his gentleman's gentleman Harold (George Rose), "poor in the only real sense of the word, sir, in that you will not be rich." Staked to six weeks' expenses by his scheming uncle (James Coco), Henry sets out to marry back into money. He finds a suitable mate in Henrietta Lowell, the hapless botanist daughter of "an industrialist. Or a composer, something like that." As Henry says, "Never have I seen one woman in whom every social grace was so lacking." Before the marriage certificate is signed, he's plotting her demise. But fate has other plans. Many other plans.

Lawyer Jack Weston counsels the allegedly happy couple of Matthau and writer/director Elaine May in *A New Leaf*.

A perverse romantic angle drew May to Jack Ritchie's 1963 short story "The Green Heart." In an interview following a screening of *A New Leaf* at the 2013 Austin Film Festival, May said, "halfway through it, you understand that the guy who was going to murder the woman really loved her and didn't know it, and you read the story and thought, 'Oh, he's not going to know it in time.'" Matthau called May's script "fast, fresh, and on a kind of literary plane which may or may not work. I think it will." He expressed reservations about May taking on too many responsibilities, a fear that would be borne out. May biographer Shawn Levy wrote that she shot some scenes as many as thirty times "as if working on improv sketches" of the kind that made her reputation in comedy. The film went six weeks over schedule. May edited the footage for ten months, finally submitting a version that ran almost three hours. The film was recut without her input, with May ultimately suing Paramount to have her name removed from the released version, a legal battle she lost.

At the core of the dispute was May's fidelity to the source material's noir nature. In Ritchie's story, Henry discovers that his bride is the target of a blackmailer (played in the film by William Hickey, whose role was excised completely) while also being extorted by her own attorney (Jack Weston). Henry murders both men in advance of killing his wife. At the 2013 Austin Film Festival, May described the sequence of Matthau watching Weston "drink poisoned scotch for just like ten minutes" as "one of the funniest scenes I've ever seen . . . I said, 'What were you playing?' And [Matthau] said, 'I was playing that when he died, I was going to eat him.'" Henry's decision to spare Henrietta—treating marriage as punishment for his crimes—was essential to May's vision; in her lawsuit against Paramount, she stated, "I made a film about a man who commits two murders and gets away with it." Now, Henry's misguided mercy is presented as a happy ending.

Still, the bastardized version of *A New Leaf* remains one of the brightest comedies of its decade. Matthau might seem an incongruous casting choice; surely Henry Graham would require the suave urbanity of a George Sanders or Macready. But the lack of a to-the-manor-born manner only makes Matthau's grim determination funnier, as in the honeymoon scene when Henry studies a guide to poisons so intently he doesn't notice that Henrietta, in pursuit of a rare plant specimen, nearly tumbles to her death. (Matthau and May would again play husband and wife in the 1978 film adaptation of Neil Simon's *California Suite*.)

May's script was nominated for the Writers Guild of America award for Best Comedy Adapted from Another Medium. She lost to John Paxton, whose many noir credits include *Murder, My Sweet* (1944) and *Crossfire* (1947). He won for *Kotch* (1971), the sole film directed by Jack Lemmon. Its star? Walter Matthau, earning his second Academy Award nomination.

"NO SUCH THING AS WORRYING TOO MUCH."

Charley Varrick the movie and Charley Varrick the character both raise efficiency to the level of art. A stunt pilot turned crop duster, Charley (Matthau) makes ends meet with the occasional bank robbery. Competence ratchets up the tension in the opening heist sequence: Charley's crew wiping off their fingerprints amid the frenzy of the job, an eagle-eyed cop spotting a hot license plate. When the shooting stops, Charley and the sole surviving member of his team, Harman (Andrew Robinson), have netted over three-quarters of a million dollars from a dusty New Mexico bank that should have held a few thousand bucks at most. While Harman celebrates, Charley immediately checks to see if their surprise windfall is counterfeit. Confirming that it's not, he correctly surmises that they've knocked over a Mafia drop. Harman still doesn't see the problem, even as Charley warns "I'd rather have ten FBIs after me." To survive, Charley sets in motion a risky plan that will require the nerve to show his hand, leaving a trail for his pursuers on both sides of the law to follow—particularly the relentless hit man Molly, memorably played by Joe Don Baker.

Matthau hardly seems like anyone's first choice to play a steely criminal. And he wasn't; director Don Siegel hoped to reunite with frequent collaborator Clint Eastwood, and when he passed Universal pursued Donald Sutherland for the role. But Matthau takes control of the movie at once, notably with Charley's flicker of genuine grief when his wife, Nadine (Jacqueline Scott), dies of a wound sustained during the rob-

Director Don Siegel, here with actor Andrew Robinson, believed Matthau's comments about *Charley Varrick* hurt the film at the box office.

Charley Varrick the movie and Charley Varrick the character both prize efficiency.

bery. His mourning doesn't last; with no sentiment, he disposes of her body in order to aid his and Harman's escape. Matthau establishes Charley's heart and his pragmatism, both vital to the movie, in a matter of seconds. His presence occasionally seems incongruous—when Sheree North's photographer calls him a handsome man, you can't help thinking, *Him?*—but Matthau uses that to his advantage. Charley bluffs his way into the home of the bank president's secretary (Felicia Farr) to acquire information. He eyes her circular bed and idly asks which direction is best for sleeping, capping the conversation with "What I had in mind was boxing the compass." Eastwood would have tossed off the line easily. Matthau, the gifted farceur, puts the dialogue in quotes, Charley hoping that confidence will carry the day. Surprise, surprise, it does. The genius of Matthau's casting becomes apparent at the end, when Charley's bold gambit has succeeded. He's come out on top, with a fortune in his hands. But watch his walk in those final moments. It's the walk of a man on his way home to a cold dinner after a long day, the trudge of someone who works for a living. *Charley Varrick*, the man and the movie, are about getting the job done.

What's astounding is how much effort the actor put into *not* playing the role. According to Siegel, "Matthau was the only person I knew who did not like the script," adapted by Dean Riesner and Howard A. Rodman from John Reese's novel *The Looters* (1968). It is a marvel of construction, with no element going to waste: Harman's toothache, a throwaway reference to the drunk act Charley performed back when he was wooing Nadine. Even the suspicion harbored by Charley's neighbor that their milkman is a pervert pays off. Matthau didn't care for the screenplay's craftsmanship, dismissing it as "the worst thing I've ever read in my life" in a *Los Angeles Times* interview. Siegel reported receiving an audio cassette from Matthau recounting his criticisms and offering suggestions, like a framing device in which Charley spills his story to a psychiatrist or pitches the caper to a movie executive because, Matthau insisted, "there should be a device which explains what is happening." Siegel summarized their difference of opinion in his autobiography *A Siegel Film* (1993): "Walter wants to see the banana *before* he slips on it."

Matthau likely felt that he was material ill-suited for the material; during production, he asked Robinson, "Why am I in this movie? I'm terrible in this." Upon its release, the actor doubled down on his disdain. During *Charley Varrick*'s promotional junket, Carolyn Clay of the *Boston Globe* noted that Matthau was more interested in the New York Mets' chances in the World Series. (As Matthau stated "I will invariably bet on a loser," it's a certainty he went all in on the Amazins.) The film had already opened to acclaim in the UK—Matthau would win a BAFTA Award for his performance—but the actor commented on those reviews to Clay "dubiously." He described the film as "totally immoral. It just isn't viciously immoral" and heaped scorn on his "gratuitous" love scene with Farr: "They dragged that bedroom into the movie like a wet cat into a meeting of the Security Council—because it sells."

"I felt (Matthau's) attitude seriously hurt the profits," Siegel wrote. "He was, to a large extent, responsible for the studio's lack of interest in *Charley Varrick*. If a studio doesn't get behind the selling of the picture, you might as well not make it." Siegel bet Matthau over a thousand dollars that a film the actor made prior to *Charley Varrick* would outgross it. He sent Matthau a check to cover the debt, which the actor returned. Matthau preferred to wait five years for a full reckoning of *Charley Varrick*'s financial fate, as attuned to the details as the man he played.

"IT'S A ROTTEN BUSINESS, YOU NEVER SEE ANYTHING GOOD."

Matthau's next two noir-adjacent films could have been underwritten by the original Big Three automakers; in each he plays a detective investigating violence that erupts on public transit. *The Laughing Policeman* is based on the 1971 book by Maj Sjöwall and Per Wahlöö. The married authors, in their landmark ten novels featuring Detective Martin Beck (of which *The Laughing Policeman* is the fourth), set out to "portray Swedish society from a distinctly Marxist perspective . . . clothed in the garments of a police procedural," according to Wendy Lesser in her survey *Scandinavian Noir* (2020). There's scant Marxism in the film, shrewdly transplanted to San Francisco by screenwriter Thomas Rickman and director Stuart Rosenberg. But it remains faithful to the novel's spirit, depicting the police force as a cumbersome institution, slow to adapt at the best of times, wholly at sea during an era of social upheaval. The individual cops are plodders, uninspired but dogged, "We're working the case" their constant refrain. Matthau, as the Beck surrogate Jake Martin, describes police work as waiting for

Matthau's detective and his partner, Bruce Dern, in *The Laughing Policeman*.

The action of Maj Sjöwall and Per Wahlöö's novel was transplanted from Sweden to San Francisco.

someone to come in and tell them who did it, and later startles his fellow detectives—and the audience—by voicing a fatalistic sentiment: "Let's find out who the killer is before he commits suicide and then we'll never know."

The killer in this case is responsible for a massacre on a city bus. One of the victims is Martin's partner, Dave Evans, supposedly on vacation. The movie approximates the dispassionate tone of the Sjöwall-Wahlöö novels, evident in the way the bodies at the crime scene are handled, the grinding of metal as the wrecked bus is towed away. But it also conjures a tense atmosphere all its own, with a clear sense of the Zodiac killings still hanging over San Francisco.

Martin's complex homelife is presented without elaboration. He and his wife lead cordial but largely separate existences under the same roof, the job partly but not entirely to blame: "You work in the gutter, you never see anything good," he explains to her. During the investigation, he spots his teenage son at a Mitchell Brothers–style pornography theater, setting up a confrontation between them that never comes. Jazz burbles out of transistor radios or car stereos wherever Martin is, a quietly insistent way of asserting his presence and marking his territory.

The Laughing Policeman shows the detectives struggling to deal with San Francisco's Black and LGBTQ residents, with Martin being the best of the lot in that he at least acknowledges the city's transformation and the need for the department to adapt. Still, he's far from perfect. He slaps Evans's girlfriend, Kay (Cathy Lee Crosby), after discovering provocative photographs of her, not only because they lead him to realize that one of his own failures prompted Evans's murder, but also because he doesn't comprehend consent, the idea that Kay might willingly pose for such photos. With its quotidian depiction of law enforcement, the film serves as the antithesis to *Dirty Harry* (1971), a film Matthau had passed on—and disparaged on his *Charley Varrick* press tour, despite its being directed by Don Siegel.

In a 1967 interview, Matthau said, "I am afraid when I ride the subway," regularly projecting

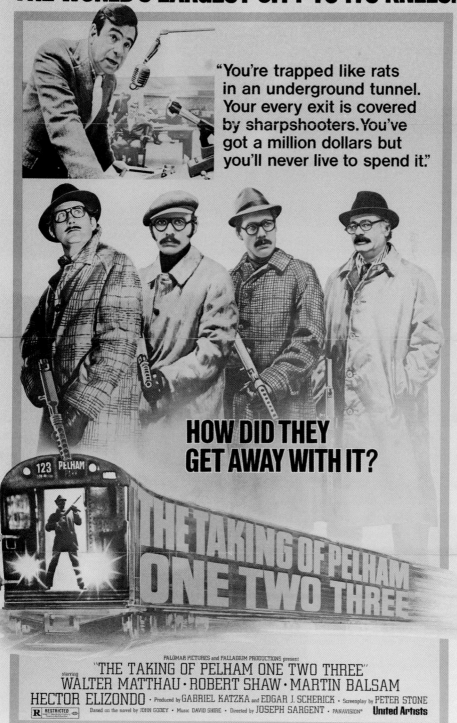

Matthau's transit cop Zachary Garber oversees the worst commute in New York City history in *The Taking of Pelham One Two Three*.

the image of a detective to compensate. The acting exercise would come in handy for *The Taking of Pelham One Two Three*, possibly the most New York movie ever made. Filmed during the darkest days of the Big Apple's "Fun City" phase, it posits every commuter's worst nightmare: a subway car full of passengers held for ransom by merciless criminals. The film knows that the dominant emotion of New York is not excitement but exasperation, and it sings an aria of irritation. Sure, a brilliantly planned and executed crime is taking place beneath the streets of Manhattan, but how is it going to affect rush hour?

Peter Stone, who wrote *Mirage*, beautifully adapted the 1973 novel by John Godey (pseudonym for former studio publicist Morton Freedgood), consolidating several characters into Matthau's transit cop Lieutenant

Pelham filmed in and around the subway system in Brooklyn, with Matthau's hideous yellow necktie often taking center stage.

Zachary Garber. When a 6 train from the Bronx is seized by gunmen led by Robert Shaw's Mr. Blue, Garber must negotiate with them—or, in the words of frustrated trainmaster Frank Correll (Dick O'Neill), to play "grabass with a bunch of friggin' pirates." After all, Correll's got a subway to run.

Matthau praised the speed of Stone's script and does nothing to slow its tempo, letting his wardrobe—a garish plaid shirt accessorized with a nauseating yellow necktie—do much of the work. Producer Edgar J. Scherick told the *New York Times* that the film's "heroes represent the positive forces in our society," but Garber is hardly a conventional role model. He adds "meshuggaas" to the litany of crimes committed in the subway when leading a tour for his Tokyo counterparts, and dismisses a six-figure bribe with, "My accountant says I've accepted enough for this fiscal quarter."

During the arduous shoot in and around Brooklyn's abandoned Court Street station, Matthau acquired "the strangest cold I ever had," resulting in him losing his voice for several days, and he told reporters he'd seen a bug in the tunnels mug a guy. He got along well with costar Shaw, the two trading jokes and Shaw saluting Matthau "as the better drinker." *The Taking of Pelham One Two Three* is graced with one of the few flawless endings in film, a sublime reaction shot of Matthau that lives on in memes today. Matthau's son Charles, a filmmaker who directed his father several times, inspired that moment, telling biographers Rob Edelman and Audrey Kupferberg that the priceless expression that closes the film is Matthau *père*'s version of Matthau *fils*'s Charlie Chaplin impression.

Matthau returned to more familiar ground, largely sticking to comedy, his occasional forays into the shadows tinged with laughs, as in *Hopscotch* (1980), or alleged laughs in the case of Billy Wilder's woeful swan song *Buddy Buddy* (1981). He wouldn't make a straight crime film again. But after the early 1970s, he didn't need to. ■

JEAN HAGEN'S TRAIL OF BROKEN DREAMS

Steve Kronenberg

She's best known for her Oscar-nominated performance as the daffy but devious Lina Lamont in *Singin' in the Rain* (1952). But that role is only a part of Jean Hagen's cinematic legacy. She left an indelible mark on film noir, portraying women cursed by bad luck, bad breaks, and bad men.

Born in Chicago on August 3, 1923, Jean Shirley Verhagen answered the call of the stage at an early age. "I always wanted to be an actress," she once said. As a child, she and her sister, Laverne, performed plays in the basement of their home. "We wrote them and acted in them and charged five cents," Jean recalled. She studied drama at Northwestern University, where she forged a lifelong bond with her roommate, Patricia Neal. Her ambition and talent were nurtured in little theater groups, on radio, and Broadway, where she appeared in plays by Lillian Hellman and Charles MacArthur and Ben Hecht. Her penchant for brass and sass flowered when she understudied and later replaced Judy Holliday on stage in *Born Yesterday*.

In 1949, while on location for his New York noir *Side Street* (1950), Anthony Mann caught Hagen's performance in Herman Wouk's play *The Traitor*. The impressed director offered her a role in the picture, which she eagerly accepted. Hagen's work in film—and film noir—began with *Side Street*, though moviegoers first saw her as flagrant floozy Beryl Caighn in *Adam's Rib* (1949), which was released five months before Mann's film.

Blue Jean: Hagen warbles a sorrowful song as sad chanteuse Harriet Sinton in *Side Street*.

Hagen's debut in *Side Street* is as auspicious as it is assured. Farley Granger and Cathy O'Donnell, reunited after their collaboration in *They Live by Night* (1948), play Joe and Ellen Norson, a young couple with a baby on the way, living penuriously off Joe's meager salary as a postman. While on a postal run, Joe furtively steals what he thinks is $200 from the office of a mob attorney (Edmon Ryan). He doesn't realize he's inadvertently pilfered $30,000 in blood money belonging to vicious gangster Georgie Garsell (James Craig). The theft plunges Joe into a whirlpool, spinning him from a phony murder rap to a final confrontation with Garsell. Enter Jean Hagen as Harriet Sinton, nightclub singer and Garsell's main squeeze. Determined to clear his name and lead the cops to Garsell, Joe tracks Harriet down at her club gig. She deceptively entices him before delivering him to her murderous lover, who plans to eliminate Joe as a loose end. Hagen doesn't play Harriet as just another shady chanteuse. She bears the psychic scars of a life lived on the edge, accepting drinks from Joe and slowly slipping into a pitiful mix of booze and bamboozle. As a sham seductress, Hagen's act within an act works, deceiving both Joe and the audience. "You got real nice manners, Joe," she whispers, using her sad eyes and pursed, pouting lips to beguile Joe with poetry while revealing the beatings she's received from Garsell. "He hit me once when I recited Robert Burns," she sighs. "He hit me right in the eye." Hagen allows some verve to peek through the vulnerability. She angrily upbraids a waiter who calls her by her first name: "I'm not one of the help. You call me *Miss Sinton*." She exudes sexual tension,

On location at the Ben Eubank farm in Kentucky, Hagen reviews her script before filming the final scene in *The Asphalt Jungle*. Accompanying her are Mrs. James Steele, standing left; Mrs. Ben Eubank Jr., standing right; and Mrs. Sterling Hayden, seated right.

melting into Joe's arms as she lures him to Garsell's apartment, where the sadistic hood repays her loyalty by strangling her. Harriet is *Side Street*'s femme fatale, but Hagen imbues her with humility and heartbreak, delivering the film's most interesting and nuanced performance. It's also the role that would serve as a template for the pathos and passion she would continue to bring to film noir.

John Huston insisted on casting Hagen as Doll Conovan in *The Asphalt Jungle* (1950) "because she has a wistful, down-to-earth quality rare on the screen. A born actress." (He also sought Hagen's advice before choosing Marilyn Monroe to play Angela Phinlay.) Hagen's scenes with Sterling Hayden's Dix Handley are suffused with pain and pathos. We meet her as she wearily climbs the stairs to Dix's shabby apartment, newly unemployed after the cheap club she sang at was raided. Her face is worn by the scum and scrum of the city, and we empathize with her heartache: the way she clumsily removes her false eyelashes, betraying a childlike embarrassment as she struggles with them; her goofy, endearing chuckle when she tells Dix that her club was raided on pay night; how she listens raptly when Dix describes his boyhood home in Kentucky. Locked out of her job and home, her teary eyes implore Dix for a place to crash: "I've never had a proper home . . . just for a couple of nights," she begs. Her desperation is palpable, and Dix gives in with a grin. Later, she pathetically takes a diamond from Dix's stolen stash and puts it on her ring finger, momentarily living an unfulfilled dream. Doll loves Dix, and while he stops short of returning her affection, her love isn't exactly unrequited. When he's with her, he's a softer, gentler man and he knows it; the hardened gunsel is touched by her devotion. Hagen's scenes with Hayden are a master class in naturalism. They're also linked to the film's thematic clash between hubris and humanism.

Doll isn't all sadness and servility. Hagen explores a wide emotional arc, treading between joy, sorrow, and determination. After Doll finds a car for the mortally wounded Dix to flee to Kentucky, he tells her she can't accompany him. Cinematographer Harold Rosson's camera captures Doll in closeup, her face taut as she delivers a stern ultimatum: she rides along or she won't tell him where the car is. He relents and allows her to gently nurse his gunshot wound before seeking medical assistance. Throughout these scenes, Hagen controls Doll's distress: she's frightened and fretful, but she never overplays her anguish, even during the movie's tragic finale, as she quietly sobs while Dix bleeds to death.

"In *The Asphalt Jungle*, there are two women," Hagen joked. "Me and Marilyn Monroe. And I'm not Marilyn Monroe!" Monroe provides the sexual splash, but Hagen's performance is endowed with an unalloyed truth. She eases into Doll's persona with confidence, seizing it and squeezing from it every drop of poignancy and despair.

No Questions Asked (1951) is a pulpy but serviceable noir enriched by Hagen's affecting performance as Joan Brenson, hopelessly in love with corrupt insurance company lawyer Steve Keiver (Barry Sullivan). Keiver hatches a scheme to sell stolen goods back to his employer with "no questions asked." He shares the proceeds with some low-level crooks, but his real motivation is keeping glamorous girlfriend Ellen Sayburn (Arlene Dahl) in diamonds and furs. Dahl's duplicitous gold digger is all glitz and gloss, but it's Hagen who delivers the film's most impressive work, informed by a combination of gravitas and yearning. "Maybe I'm sticking around with you because you're a haunted guy," Joan tells Keiver. "Maybe I'm just waiting for the ghost to come back." Her eyes turn mournful as she spots a photo of Ellen on Keiver's mantle. When she learns that Keiver intends to marry Ellen, Joan adopts the look of a defeated woman, her face a picture of dejection. She's one tear away from a breakdown, but Hagen keeps her emotions in check. In a key scene, Joan dines alone, gets drunk, and gracefully glides to a jukebox to croon a lovely, lovelorn cover of "I've Got You Under My Skin." (When *Singin' in the Rain* concludes, that's Hagen's beautiful voice singing the title tune, double dubbing both Debbie Reynolds and herself.) Joan Brenson is one of Hagen's most controlled and sympathetic portrayals, rivaling Doll Conovan. "It is Jean Hagen who is responsible for the one real performance in the picture," lauded the *New York Herald-Tribune*.

In 1953, Hagen shifted to the small screen to play Margaret Williams, Danny Thomas's wife in the popular sitcom *Make Room for Daddy* (1953–65). Though she infused the role with an independent

The Hagen-Hayden dynamic is one of many highlights in *The Asphalt Jungle*.

streak, the daily grind of series television left her bored and exhausted. The monotony was compounded by Thomas, who derided her for refusing to wear makeup and heels while offstage. After three seasons and three Emmy nominations, Hagen quit the show in 1956. In an unprecedented move, an angry Thomas demanded that her character be killed off and replaced.

The tedium of television was somewhat salved when Hagen was cast in *The Big Knife* (1955). "Honestly, this is the part that saved my sanity," she told writer Ray Hagen (no relation). Jack Palance is Charlie Castle, a depressed film star fed up with Hollywood. He's torn between his supportive wife (Ida Lupino), who wants him to retire, and an explosive studio boss (Rod Steiger) urging him to continue cranking out cash cows. Hagen plays Connie Bliss, a feral, whiskey-soaked nymphomaniac whose only goal is to join Castle for a night in the sack. Bumping and grinding, she sashays her way to his bedroom. "Tequila always makes me frisky," she sighs, blowing in his ear and waving a back scratcher in his face. She uses her winning smile and provocative body language to tease Castle into bed, but Hagen melds Connie's carnality with a sense of sorrow and desolation. When Castle violently pushes her away before succumbing to her, Connie's masochism and melancholy descend on her. "That hurts, boyfriend," she purrs. "I wish I could say I didn't like it." The picture's noir cred is debatable, but Hagen hands us the film's most genuine performance, comfortably coupling sexuality and sympathy.

When Hagen left *Make Room for Daddy*, she abandoned a role with which she'd become inseparably identified. Film offers dried up and she slipped into depression. "All of a sudden she had nothing to do," recalled her daughter, Christine. "That's when she started to drink." Ironically, television sustained her career, with guest appearances in live dramas and long-running series. NOIR CITY dwellers should sample her work in "Enough Rope for Two," a hardboiled episode of *Alfred Hitchcock Presents* (1955–62) that originally aired on November 17, 1957. Hagen is up to no good as Madge Griffin, part of a trio out to recover $100,000 stolen in a payroll heist by ex-con Joe Kedzie (Steven Hill) and his partner, Maxie (Steve Brodie). Joe has hidden the loot in a desert mine shaft, and the threesome plan to find it and split it—but Madge is less interested in splitting it than splitting *with* it. Within her scant 20-minute screen time, Hagen segues from soft to sinister, playing Joe and Maxie against each other while planning a deadly double cross. Her subtle shifts in mood and manner keep us guessing until the delightfully diabolical denouement.

No longer a compliant TV wife, Hagen confronted the dark side of domesticity in *Panic in Year Zero!* (1962), a dystopian "nuke noir" directed by and costarring Ray Milland. She and Milland play Ann and Harry Baldwin who, with their son (Frankie Avalon) and daughter (Mary Mitchel), survive a nuclear attack and fight to stay alive in its aftermath. Hagen is reserved and controlled as a wife who defies her husband's refusal to help fellow survivors. "What do you want to do," Ann asks Harry. "Write off the rest of the world?" Hagen is much more than a supporting player; she's the conscience and counterpoint to Milland's flinty persona and gun-toting vigilantism. Stolid and steady, she complements the movie's mounting sense of dread and desperation. During filming, Mitchel noticed Hagen's melancholic state and tried reaching out to her. Hagen simply told her she was "mourning the loss of a loved one." She may have been speaking about herself.

By 1965, Hagen's alcoholism had become uncontrollable. Her condition intensified after a bitter divorce cost her the custody of her two children. In 1968, she lapsed into a coma while hospitalized for alcohol poisoning. She recovered, reunited with her daughter, and never drank again. No sooner had she conquered alcoholism than she began battling esophageal cancer. She remained upbeat while attempting to find a cure for the disease, bonding with friends Patricia Neal and Helen Thomson. During this difficult time, her sense of humor remained unfazed. When Thomson asked her how movie stars disposed of their trash, Hagen replied: "We wrap it in a fur coat and throw it off a cliff." As her cancer worsened, she was admitted to the Motion Picture and Television Country Home and Hospital, where she died on August 29, 1977, at age fifty-four.

Jean Hagen's ability to embrace a character, to veer between sin and sadness, marks her as one of noir's finest actors. What's truly remarkable is how she made it all look so damn easy. ■

NOIR BY ANY NAME

THE CRIME DRAMAS OF BOB RAFELSON

Peter Tonguette

One of the first things Bob Rafelson told me was that he did not make, care for, or wish to discuss film noir.

It was the summer of 2004, and I was a twenty-one-year-old budding film critic and journalist. Bob was the seventy-one-year-old filmmaker responsible for several films that helped define and energize the New Hollywood movement, including his signature collaborations with Jack Nicholson—*Five Easy Pieces* (1970) and *The King of Marvin Gardens* (1972).

Prior to meeting Bob, I'd seen and admired what turned out to be his last film, *No Good Deed* (2003). Although no masterpiece, it was, to my thinking, the latest in a series of expertly crafted, uniquely malicious noirs, a form in which Bob had come to specialize since his star had fallen: *The Postman Always Rings Twice* (1981), *Black Widow* (1987), *Blood and Wine* (1997), and *Poodle Springs* (1998).

A skillful adaptation (and modernization) of Dashiell Hammett's short story "The House in Turk Street" (1924), *No Good Deed* starred Samuel L. Jackson as Jack Friar, a detective who comes to regret his offer to find a friend's missing teenage daughter. His off-duty sleuthing leads to Jack being kidnapped by a motley gang of crooks, including a beautiful pianist with a severed toe, played by Milla Jovovich. As it happens, Jack is a cellist, and in the film's best moment, he makes music with his captor. "The business of the romance being articulated through music by the conjoining of cello and piano, that was, I think, my contribution," Rafelson told me.

I had contacted the director because I was disgusted by the cursory release of *No Good Deed*, which was dumped into about four hundred multiplexes in mid-September 2003. The one in my town was virtually empty when I saw it on opening day. Released without press screenings, the film grossed a meager $127,000 its opening weekend. Then it vanished.

Jessica Lange's smoldering career-changing role as Cora in *The Postman Always Rings Twice* (1981).

The intensity of the central relationship in the film led to a memorable tag line on the poster: "You will feel the heat."

It could be argued that no other contemporary American director with comparable credentials committed himself so thoroughly to the literature of noir; Rafelson had already made films from works by James M. Cain and Raymond Chandler (*Poodle Springs* was unfinished at the time of the author's death, and was later completed by Robert B. Parker). Between those canonical adaptations, he had either pursued or initiated original scripts in a neo-noir vein: *Black Widow* was written by Ron Bass, and *Blood and Wine* was co-written by Nick Villiers and Alison Cross from a story by Villiers and Rafelson. Now added to the list was a more than respectable translation of Hammett. Given Rafelson's pedigree as a maker of "art" films, his sudden turn to genre material struck me as impressive—yet no one seemed to care.

When I contacted the director to suggest an interview about his interest in noir, he flatly denied any such interest. After several emails, I finally heard from him: "I do not want to discuss all the previous so-called noirs," he wrote, using his preferred term for the genre: "so-called noirs." "I haven't seen them since I made them. I can't put them into a genre." *But he'd adapted works by the three undisputed masters of the form.* "I know I am probably the only one to do Hammett, Cain and Chandler," he wrote. "Nonetheless, I'm not fond of the genre."

Eventually, Bob agreed to an interview. The scope was both enlarged and narrowed from what I had originally proposed. According to the terms set by Bob, the interview would not be limited to his "so-called noirs" but would encompass his entire career, starting with The Monkees and his directorial debut, the gleefully deranged *Head* (1968), continuing with the international triumph of *Five Easy Pieces*, and traipsing, ever so gingerly, through what I still regarded as his rich noir period.

Rafelson felt that Jack Nicholson would have a career comparable to John Garfield, star of the MGM version of *The Postman Always Rings Twice* (1946).

Rafelson, Nicholson, Lange, and cinematographer Sven Nykvist on location.

Bob was willing to discuss it all, but he also wanted the interview to mostly focus on *No Good Deed*, which he considered to be a neglected and underappreciated film. While he feigned nonchalance about his work, in truth the director cared deeply that his films were seen and acknowledged.

Rafelson's sharp edges and wicked sense of humor did not alarm me. As I got the measure of him through our conversations, I came to feel that he had the ideal—perhaps even the exemplary—sensibility for noir: he could be adversarial, combative, attuned to dark ironies, perfect for being the chief cinematic expositor of Hammett, Cain, and Chandler, even if he could never quite bring himself to admit it.

"Bob didn't like talking about his own movies much, especially around his dinner table," said Gabrielle Rafelson, Bob's second wife. "But I think Bob was drawn to the noir genre because [the stories] were dirty, complicated, and sexy. It intrigued him to see flawed characters get rattled and twisted around by unforeseen circumstances that caused them to behave in an extreme manner."

Rafelson framed his alleged interest in noir in much the same manner: as a means to an end. He told me that he had difficulty understanding why plots were important in movies; characters were what interested him. No one who saw his episodic early movies would have trouble believing this. In *Five Easy Pieces*, we do not remember the narrative as much as the little incidents along the way: Nicholson contending with an inflexible waitress or being unable to control his emotions when speaking to his mute, infirm father.

"I think one of the reasons why I have made some noir films, *so-called* noir films," Rafelson said, "is because they come with plots." A sharp insight: the noir stories he adapted were already elaborately plotted, which let Bob off the hook of having to dream them up himself. "The characters are much less interesting to me in those writings than the stories, but the characters are left to me to flesh out and to invent," he explained.

Nonetheless, the fact remains that complex, well-constructed plots exist in genres other than noir. Rafelson could just as easily have turned his attention to, say, the spy novels of John le Carré. Instead, he chose noir. It could not have been by accident.

Yet Bob made it clear that he had backed into the genre. In 1979, he'd endeavored to direct a prison drama for 20th Century-Fox, *Brubaker*—the first picture he'd attempted outside the partnership he forged with Bert Schneider, with whom he'd made *Five Easy Pieces* and *The King of Marvin Gardens*.

Brubaker represented a final break with the Schneider period—and the experience nearly broke Rafelson. The director who prided himself on pushing the limits of conventional behavior finally crossed the line in a controversial confrontation with a studio executive, leading to his immediate dismissal from the picture. Much fallout followed.

"I had been in a rough time of not making a picture for a number of years because I had presumably beaten up the head of a studio and gone through a lawsuit," he told me. Needing to resuscitate his career, Rafelson was approached by Jack Nicholson about making a fresh adaptation of *The Postman Always Rings Twice*, previously made at MGM in 1946. Nicholson had mistakenly assumed Rafelson had long wanted to remake the film.

"I said, 'No, I wasn't truly interested in making that picture, Jack. You misunderstood. I told you at one point early on that I thought your career would resemble John Garfield's and that you had something in common with him in that you could play peripheral characters who lived on the margins of society as opposed to a central leading man.'"

The director, who hired playwright David Mamet to adapt Cain's novel, felt Nicholson was well-suited to play Frank Chambers, the reprobate drifter who's hired on at a diner only to have a torrid entanglement with Cora, the wife of the proprietor.

Rafelson had definite ideas about the brutality and passion with which he wanted to tell the tale. He spoke dismissively of the 1946 film; its qualities of honest craftsmanship eluded Bob. "Here was this backwoods kind of girl working in a diner, played by Lana Turner, and her introduction is in a white dress with a white turban, hardly the kind of garb a girl working in a diner would be wearing," he said.

Instead of the glamorous Turner, Rafelson cast the naturalistic, unfussy, utterly sensuous Jessica Lange, whose scant screen appearances to date included the 1976 remake of *King Kong*. By this time Rafelson was divorced from his first wife, production designer Toby Carr Rafelson, but she remembers Bob seeking her input on the casting of Cora.

"He had me look at various auditions . . . including Jessica Lange," she says. "I think he showed

The Rafelson version of Cain's novel is defined by its emotional intensity.

me some kind of an interview he did with her, but he also showed me some of her scenes in *King Kong*. After seeing those, I said to him, 'I think she's the one out of all the people you've shown me.' He said, 'What makes you think that?' I said, 'She's a great screamer.' In other words, it didn't matter what the quality of the material was, or how cheap or how sensational it was. She could do it better than anybody else."

Lange was utterly credible as a woman whose discontent was so profound that she allows herself to be seduced by a stupid and boorish man who could only be attractive in comparison to her husband. Within the stifling context of her domestic life, Cora finds an outlet for her desperate intensity in her affair with Frank, displayed graphically in the infamous sex scene atop a kitchen table dusted in flour. Bob said that the scene was so widely discussed "it commenced a rush on cooking lessons."

Anjelica Huston, then Nicholson's companion, had a memorable early role in the picture as a lion tamer with whom Frank has a dalliance. She recalled the relationship between Rafelson and Nicholson as "brotherly." "It was friendly, loving, a little bit challenging," Huston says. "What did Jack call Bob? He had some name for him. 'Curly.' He had a nickname for everyone. 'Curly Bob.' Bob was always a little irritated with Jack about something. I remember Jack gave him a toilet seat for one Christmas. That really irritated Bob, and he took me to task for it, which I found quite insulting since I would never have presumed to give him a toilet seat!" She adds: "There was a certain amount of joshing and fun. They liked to go on adventures, and they would climb mountains and ski a lot."

Bob insisted to me that he saw *The Postman Always Rings Twice* not as a noir but as a love story with tragic contours. He instructed cinematographer Sven Nykvist to refrain from obvious noir imagery. What he wanted from Nykvist was "the loving way he used light" to photograph women's faces for Ingmar Bergman.

Even so—except for a crucial omission to the ending that, in Bob's mind, solidified its status as a wrecked romance rather than an ironic moral tale—the film is true to the essence of Cain's plot, including the twist that, by definition, makes it noir: Cora schemes with Frank to kill her husband, a plot the two execute blunderingly before pulling it off successfully. Rafelson's raw and fierce version of the story is not only a noir but one that, using the freedom of a well-deserved R rating, realizes its author's story with maximum impact. With so much evidence to the contrary, why did Rafelson keep saying that he didn't think his noirs were noirs?

Theresa Russell as a serial killer of a succession of husbands in *Black Widow*.

Jack Nicholson and Michael Caine costar in the neo-noir *Blood and Wine*.

"Sometimes people don't really want to be identified in any way," Toby Carr Rafelson says. "They don't want to be labeled, they don't want to have somebody from the outside tell them that's who they are. Maybe Bob found that a limiting definition."

Never again would Rafelson match the combination of ardor and violence he brought to *The Postman Always Rings Twice*—but he'd found the form that would see him through to the conclusion of his career. In 1987, he made *Black Widow*, starring Theresa Russell as a serial killer, Catharine Petersen. Her targets were wealthy men who could be easily disposed of and whose bank accounts could be readily drained. Debra Winger costarred as a federal investigator who ingratiates herself with the suspected killer in much the same manner Catharine does her prey. Bob explained that he was intrigued by the theme of "the hunter and the hunted . . . being enamored of one another" applying to two women. Seen today, the film seems to pull its punches in what could have been a more intense relationship between Russell and Winger, but it is propelled by Rafelson's instinctive lack of faith in the goodness of people. There is great wit in the speed with which the various husbands—among them Nicol Williamson and Dennis Hopper—are dispatched.

About a decade later, after detours into historical drama (*Mountains of the Moon* [1990]) and comedy (*Man Trouble* [1992]), Rafelson scrutinized his own demons to produce an original neo-noir, *Blood and Wine*. Jack Nicholson plays Alex Gates, a past-his-prime wine dealer who plans a jewel heist with an even more visibly ailing cohort, Victor (Michael Caine). The film also has much to do with the strained relations between Alex and his wife (Judy Davis) and her son (Stephen Dorff), but it is a noir in the truest sense: the crime isn't the point, but the sins of those committing the crime.

"Bob was mining the depths of his experience and integrated anger, sex, and thievery into the story," says Gabrielle Rafelson. "Bob also loved wine, and he wrote with Jack in mind for the role."

Blood and Wine was produced by Jeremy Thomas, who had previously sponsored films by Bernardo Bertolucci, Nicolas Roeg, and David Cronenberg. He had known Rafelson for close to twenty years by the time *Blood and Wine* emerged as a possibility. "I saw a good noir—humorous, without a particular subtext except a continuation of work between Bob and Jack," Thomas says. "It was meant to be a very slick thriller—and grand."

James Caan offers his spin on Philip Marlowe in *Poodle Springs*.

Despite Nicholson's still-potent star power—the film came out the same year as his Oscar-winning *As Good as It Gets* (1997)—*Blood and Wine* received a cursory theatrical release and only modest box-office returns, which still chagrins its producer. "I was happy with [the film]—but not the way it was released," Thomas says. "It was maybe out of its time. It was a very good film, and I'm trying to get it reappraised. . . . It's just one of those films that maybe will get a bit more famous over the years."

In fairness, Rafelson could plausibly claim non-noir aspects in such ambitious films as *The Postman Always Rings Twice*, *Black Widow*, and *Blood and Wine*, but his final features—*Poodle Springs* and *No Good Deed*—exist solidly within the tradition he argued with. *Poodle Springs* stars James Caan as Philip Marlowe, one in a succession of rough-around-the-edges actors to inhabit Chandler's legendary detective.

In preparing the picture, cinematographer Stuart Dryburgh remembered studying another Marlowe film. "I looked at the Robert Mitchum version of *Farewell, My Lovely*—a color noir, shot by John Alonzo, a fucking gorgeous movie," Dryburgh says. "I don't think anyone has ever hit color noir better than that. It's tricky, because traditionally it is a black-and-white thing, and the colors are incredibly rich, but it still has that contrast and the Venetian blind shadows."

For *Poodle Springs*, however, Rafelson wanted to remain true to the story's mid-century setting. "What Bob made very clear was that this movie is set in the 1960s," Dryburgh says. "We needed to make sure that photographically we had a cleaner look." Yet the traditional camerawork gave the film a self-consciously noirish patina. "We stayed very much in the classic Hollywood style," he reflects.

The cinematographer also appreciated Caan's grizzled characterization. "Caan was an athlete in his youth," Dryburgh recalls. "He has, over the years, accumulated a lot of injuries. To see him get up out of a chair sometimes, you saw that whole history of injury. . . . When he got out of his chair as Marlowe, he was a little bit more spry, but he still had that slightly 'I'm not quite as young as I was.' It needs that."

Then came the ill-fated *No Good Deed*—an eminently worthwhile version of Hammett's story marred by indifference on the part of its star, Samuel L. Jackson. "I remember Bob came home after meeting with Jackson for the first time, and he was dismayed by Sam's dismissive attitude about the project—which seemed to continue through the entire shoot," Gabrielle Rafelson remembers. "I can't say why that happened, or what was going on in Sam's mind, but Bob would come back to the condo we rented completely dejected from the frustrating days. I think it was the first time Bob felt he couldn't direct an actor. Couldn't get Sam to try scenes in different ways. He carried on through with the knowledge that lost things can be fixed in the editing room."

Rafelson did not embark on *No Good Deed* thinking it would be his farewell film, but according to Gabrielle he had been discouraged by the experience and decided to call it a day. In my talks and correspondence with him over nearly twenty years, I never sensed that Bob regretted the decision. He was proud of what he had accomplished. He just refused to see himself as a maker of noirs—despite his obvious attachment to the form. The proof, however, is right there on the screen—in all the desperation, deceit, and death that define the films he made during the last quarter-century of his career.

"They're dark films, and they're about, among other things, manipulation," Toby Carr Rafelson says. "They're very much about male-female relations, and strong women. There are a lot of things that you could point to that are similar to one another thematically. I wouldn't say 'pleasant' could be applied to any of Bob's movies." ∎

Peter Tonguette is a frequent contributor to the Wall Street Journal, Washington Examiner, *and* National Review. *He is writing a biography of Peter Bogdanovich.*

BLOOD OVER THE ATLANTIC

NICK GOMEZ'S EASTERN SEABOARD TRILOGY

Rachel Walther

In the mid-nineties, Nick Gomez wrote and directed three films that are still waiting for the applause they deserve. His debut, *Laws of Gravity* (1992), made when Gomez was fresh out of the film program at SUNY Purchase, details a few days in the lives of two guys surviving outside the law in Brooklyn. It was shot in less than a month, cost less than $50,000, and is one of the best features of the last thirty years. Gomez's sophomore effort, *New Jersey Drive* (1995), is an unsparing coming-of-age story about teenagers in Newark obsessed with stealing cars—more for pleasure than for profit—and running afoul of a vicious and amoral police department. *Illtown* (1996), his third, transplants the characters and scenarios of his first two efforts into the colorful glare of south Florida, in a surreal and gentle noir that's punctuated with unrivaled brutality.

"I don't need you to fix my fucking life."

No setup, no intro, no voice-over. In *Laws of Gravity*, Gomez drops us right into a typical day for Jimmy (Peter Greene) and Jon (Adam Trese). Both men are in their late twenties and get by through selling stolen electronics, shoplifting, and other crimes of opportunity. Jimmy adopts an older-brother stance with respect to Jon, giving him some grief about a court date for a shoplifting charge that the latter is missing that day. Jon responds with kid-brother petulance:

JIMMY: What are you gonna do when they come to your door?
JON: [laughs] I just won't answer.

Cinematographer Jean de Segonzac keeps us right alongside the pair as they meander and bullshit each other; the camera a passive observer throughout. While they both subsist outside the bounds of a W-4, it's understood that Jimmy's a bit more together than Jon; he respects the line and understands how crossing it will affect his life, whereas Jon is still unwilling to acknowledge that the rules apply to him at all. Jimmy's also married—to Denise (Edie Falco), the only one in the trio with a steady job. That afternoon a friend from Florida, Frankie (Paul Schulze), shows up with some guns that need selling. If Jimmy can help find a buyer, he'll get a cut of the proceeds.

Gomez and Segonzac are so adept at folding us into Jimmy's landscape that selling the guns is just one errand on his list of to-dos. Rather than crowding the film with a tense, intricate plot, they allow the drama to bubble up naturally, scene by scene, due to the inherent friction in Jimmy and Jon's relationship and Jon's determination to avoid responsibility or criticism for his misdeeds. It's this latter trait that escalates the back-to-back confrontations with everyone around him into a permanent state of violence. Gomez ratchets up the tension by keeping the camera in the fray and within range of the next swing.

The success of the film is due in no small part to the actors. Greene is wholly at ease as Jimmy; his light and lanky frame leans back against every fence and takes possession of his small, cluttered apartment as comfortably as if it were a penthouse. Falco is equally at home in this world, portraying a woman who's secure in, rather than thwarted by, the life she's made for herself. But it is Trese who truly lights up the film with his unpredictable, charged energy. In the quiet moments between blowups, he subtly conveys the range of emotions—from pain to denial to anger—that are roiling through Jon's mind and propelling all the other characters into deeper and more serious trouble.

Laws of Gravity has endured comparisons to Martin Scorsese's *Mean Streets* (1973) given their common focus on a codependent friendship between two young men scraping by on petty crimes—one more stable and one a troublemaker. But the connections are superficial. Robert De Niro's Johnny

Actors Edie Falco and Peter Greene are completely at ease as a young couple scraping by in *Laws of Gravity*.

Boy is more of a mischievous, defiant child unwilling to grow up, whereas Trese's Jon acts immaturely out of denial and misplaced rage. He takes his frustrations out on his girlfriend rather than owning up to his shortcomings, creating a darker and more nuanced portrait than De Niro's limited screen time allows for. Scorsese's film is full of cinematic trappings like internal monologue and flashbacks; *Laws of Gravity* doesn't even have a soundtrack (aside from ambient music coming from stereos and jukeboxes), let alone interest in providing character backstories or expository dialogue.

Laws of Gravity is in many ways a simple story: people trying to stay on top of their emotions and getting by in the ways they know how. They may not have much, but it's everything to them, and it's often being threatened. By remaining content to simply depict three messy, unadorned days in the lives of Jimmy, Jon, Denise, and their friends, Gomez achieved something that remains radical and exhilarating.

"You need a reason to get shot nowadays?"

A couple of teenagers are out on a joyride late one night in Newark, New Jersey. They've stolen the car and are having a damn good time until a police trap snares them—the car's tires are shot flat and bright police lights shine into the windows. Then, without warning, bullets fly into the car and shattered glass rains down on Ronnie (Koran C. Thomas) and Jason (Sharron Corley). Ronnie is injured and taken to the ER, and Jason escapes the dragnet and makes it home unscathed. The next morning, all the news agencies are blasting *a* story, but not *the* story: the two teens supposedly shot at the cops after being ordered to surrender, and then and only then did the police return fire. The lie comes as no surprise to anyone in the neighborhood. When it's young Black men versus the police, who're the public at large going to believe?

It's the overt malice on the part of the Newark police that sets the hopeless tone of *New Jersey Drive* and directs the actions of Jason and his friends. Yes, they like to steal cars to cruise around, hang out with friends, and pick up girls. But they're far from hardened criminals. They smoke a little weed but nothing more, and a few sharp words from one of their mothers send them sulking. Unlike *Laws of Gravity*, in which law enforcement and the judicial system are relatively faceless entities, the police here are active antagonists who hunt and surveil Jason and his friends, waiting for them to step out of line so they can deliver punishment in the nearest alley. Leading this effort is Officer Roscoe (Saul Stein), a cop who is singled out, in words damning for anyone in his profession, as someone who "seems to like his job a little too much." Roscoe comes under an internal investigation for Ronnie's shooting, and once he learns that Jason was the other kid in the car that night, he's determined to get to him before the grand jury does.

Jason's home life is relatively stable—a mother (Gwen McGee) who sternly supports him while correcting his grammar; a stepfather-to-be (Robert Jason Jackson) who's neither abusive nor idiotic; a sister (Samantha Brown) who's incredulous over his nighttime escapades. Perhaps it's this stability that sets Jason just a bit apart from some of his friends. After an argument with his mother, he crashes at Midget's apartment, a raucous place, especially "when all his brothers are out of jail at the same time." Midget (Gabriel Casseus) is discouraging about Jason's "straight" plans to study auto mechanics after high school:

JASON: You think I'm gonna be on the street with you for the rest of my life, man?
MIDGET: Who you think you're gonna be working for? Some white motherfucker driving a Lexus while your ass is still taking the bus.

Midget sees how deeply the system is rigged against kids like him, and considers stealing cars a small, symbolic act of protest—a way to even the scales, if just for an evening. The more the police target him for bending the rules, the more hell-bent he is on breaking them. Jason is more numb than angry. He's simply trying to survive the next few months, especially the surprise visits from Roscoe

In *New Jersey Drive*, who is the bigger threat to society—the joyriding teenager (Sharron Corley, left) or the corrupt police officer (Saul Stein, right)?

reminding him to "remember who your friends are." Even though they put him in danger, the only thing Jason has to look forward to are those moments behind the wheel of a stolen car—brief adventures of joy and levity with his friends in a life otherwise filled with disappointments, dead-end jobs, and sudden death.

New Jersey Drive depicts a community beyond justice—one where Jason's mother is so outraged that a boy would be murdered by police that she's simply unsurprised, and one in which every kid over fifteen knows someone who has been shot by the cops. The film's opinion of the Newark police is caustic and unflinching, showing the men and women tasked with upholding the law as breaking it more egregiously than the supposed criminals. This prescient view of law enforcement, tracing how a group of wayward youths are deliberately and savagely pushed into an aggressive dynamic with an entity that targets Black communities, gives you the sense that *New Jersey Drive* could have been made two years ago rather than twenty-five.

Gomez's first two films depict wholly insular realities that his characters are unwilling or unable to escape—if they even consider it a possibility. In both Jimmy's world and Jason's, incarceration is a natural stop on the wheel of life. "Rikers" is a constant refrain—a threat, a memory, an inevitability. But while most of Jon's trouble in *Laws of Gravity* is of his own making, by not heeding Jimmy's words of caution and willfully plunging toward bad decisions, what trips up Midget and Jason are often forces beyond their control. Yes, they're living outside the law in their own way, but when the punishment is so disproportionate to the crime and meted out regardless of guilt, what's the point of trying to go straight?

"I've been dead for too long."

The only thing that matters is the ride.

A Nick Gomez Film

NEW JERSEY DRIVE

In *Illtown*, the past catches up to Dante (Michael Rapaport) and Micky (Lili Taylor).

Illtown is in many ways the opposite of its predecessors. A stylized noir with the simplified plot of a Western and the murky pace of a fever dream, it's all bright neon and soft dissolves. Dante (Michael Rapaport) and Micky (Lili Taylor) are a young couple in love who run their own business—selling heroin for D'Avalon (Tony Danza). Things are going smoothly. Until they aren't.

It all takes a left turn seemingly overnight—a runner gets out of line and is dealt with fatally, and then a batch of their product is spiked and six people end up dead from bad dope. A black cloud is hovering around Dante and Micky—and his name is Gabriel (Adam Trese), an old friend who's just gotten out of jail and is back to inflict mayhem on the couple and their enterprise. Every scene moves calmly and quietly. The Florida in *Illtown* is a pleasant, uncrowded purgatory of vacant lots, ocean vistas, and empty poolrooms, and threats are made in lowered voices after long pauses.

Trese is again the standout performer, this time backing up his character's moments of levity or cheerful dismissiveness with a bullet. Gomez staples Paul Schulze and Saul Stein are glorious as (respectively) the breezy, corrupt cop Lucas and D'Avalon's mercurial boyfriend/business partner Gunther. As Gabriel chips away at Dante and Micky's operation and sets them on the run, he employs an army of teenage mercenaries to carry out his violent agenda. Murders abound and often take place in front of mute, indifferent witnesses who then go about their business and leave the bodies out in the open. These glazed, lulling scenes amplify, rather than dampen, the film's savage brutality, as if whispering to its characters: "No need to run. You're dead already."

After *Illtown*, Gomez directed one more theatrical effort—*Drowning Mona* (2000), a black comedy scripted by Peter Steinfeld and featuring none of the themes or verve of his earlier work. But he was already pivoting his unflinching and kinetic perspective to television. In the last twenty-five years, he's directed TV movies and episodes of nearly every small-screen thriller and police procedural in production. A complete list would require its own column, but to name some highlights: *Homicide: Life on the Street* (1993–99), *Oz* (1997–2003), *The Sopranos* (1999–2007), *Law & Order: SVU* (1999–), *Robbery Homicide Division* (2002–3), *The Shield* (2002–8), *Dexter* (2006–13), *Damages* (2007–12), *Detroit 1-8-7* (2010–11), *Blue Bloods* (2010–), *Magic City* (2012–13), *Ray Donovan* (2013–20), *Gang Related* (2014), *Chicago P.D.* (2014–), and *Shades of Blue* (2016–18).

It is because Gomez fashioned such insular, gripping worlds in his auteur efforts that they hold up so well nearly thirty years on, with stories that delve into the timeless noir themes of loyalty, betrayal, and abuse of power. His self-contained communities in Brooklyn, Newark, and south Florida exist in a semblance of protection and belonging, and it's Gomez's fascination with what happens when these bonds are threatened that yielded three remarkable films, all ripe for rediscovery. ■

PRIME CUTS: MY FAVORITE NEO-NOIR
Wallace Stroby

ROLLING THUNDER

Vengeance was all the rage in the crime films of the 1970s. It was a decade heavy on bloody retribution and rough justice, found in such movies as *Death Wish* (1974), *Dirty Harry* (1971), *Walking Tall* (1973), *Rage* (1972), *Framed* (1975), *Fighting Mad* (1976), and many others. One could be forgiven for writing off John Flynn's *Rolling Thunder* (1977) as just another entry in the cycle. On the surface, it fits the bill: a Vietnam veteran goes gunning for the criminals who murdered his wife and son. But on another level, and in context, it now feels like one of the most significant films of the 1970s.

Directed by journeyman Flynn (*The Outfit* [1973], *Best Seller* [1987]), *Rolling Thunder* was one of the first films to tackle the topic of returning Vietnam veterans and the issues they faced. The story and original screenplay were written by Hollywood enfant terrible Paul Schrader, then riding high on his scripts for *The Yakuza* (1974), *Obsession* (1976), and *Taxi Driver* (1976). When *Rolling Thunder* was released, the posters proclaimed it "another shattering experience from the author of TAXI DRIVER." The two films do share a theme—a Vietnam vet turns homicidal on his return to the United States. But Travis Bickle, the troubled loser of *Taxi Driver*, is a far cry from *Rolling Thunder*'s Major Charles Rane, an Air Force officer who spent seven years in a POW camp after being shot down over North Vietnam. ("Rolling Thunder" was the code name for US air operations during the war.)

As Rane, William Devane (*Marathon Man* [1976], *Family Plot* [1976]) gives a measured and finely nuanced performance, one of the best of his career. Returning to his Texas hometown—the film is set in 1973—Rane is reunited with a young son who doesn't remember him and a wife who's in love with another man. The only one he can relate to is his fellow POW, Army Sergeant Johnny Vohden (Tommy Lee Jones, in a memorable early performance). Vohden is so twitchy and lost he makes Rane seem well-adjusted. When the plane that brings them home touches down at the airport where Vohden's wife and family are waiting, Vohden confides, "Major, I sure do hate to face all them people." "Then put your glasses on, John," Rane advises him. Sunglasses in place, they take their first steps out onto the tarmac, and back into a world they hardly recognize.

As disciplined and stoic as he tries to be, Rane has his own problems. After seven years in a cell, he can't reacclimate to his old life. He sleeps in a backyard work shed because, as his wife tells their little boy, it's "small and quiet out there." In one of the film's most disturbing scenes, Rane demonstrates how he was tortured by his captors, persuading his wife's lover (Lawrason Driscoll) to participate in the reenactment by painfully hoisting Rane's bound arms behind him. "You learn to love the rope," Rane tells him. "That's how you beat them."

Honored as a hometown hero, Rane is given a red Cadillac convertible and 2,556 silver dollars, one for each day he spent in captivity and "one for good luck." When they hear of this windfall, a quartet of depraved criminals led by the Texan (James Best) and Automatic Slim (1970s icon Luke Askew) invade Rane's home and kill his wife and son. Refusing to give up the coins, evincing the same defiance he once showed his prison guards, Rane is brutalized and, in the film's most exploitative scene, his tormentors feed his right hand into the kitchen garbage disposal.

In the hospital, Rane is furnished with a prosthetic hook that he later files to razor sharpness. Sawing down the twin barrels of a shotgun given to him by his son, he plots his revenge, reluctantly aided by the

Co-screenwriter Heywood Gould, Devane, and executive producer Lawrence Gordon relax between takes on the San Antonio location.

ROLLING THUNDER
released by American International Pictures

young waitress who wore his POW bracelet (Linda Haynes, bringing vibrant life to a thinly written role). Eventually, he recruits the newly re-upped Vohden, who's happy to flee the stifling confines of civilian life. When Rane reveals he's discovered the hideout of the men who killed his family, Vohden pauses only for a moment. "I'll just get my gear," he says.

The two head to Mexico, a pair of gringos on a death trip, and find the Texan's gang holed up in a Juarez brothel. What follows is a bloodbath of Peckinpah-esque proportions, as Rane and Vohden kill nearly a dozen men in a scene that echoes the finales of both *The Wild Bunch* (1969) and *Taxi Driver*.

Unlike most films of its type, *Rolling Thunder* is deliberately paced. It moves slowly at first, taking its time to show Rane's attempts to readjust. "I had everything worked out," he tells an Air Force psychologist (Dabney Coleman). "But nothing's going the way I planned." Anchored by Devane's performance, the first half of the film is a compelling character study. Can this battered war hero reconnect with the world, and find a redemptive new love with the young woman who idolizes him? Can he rekindle the humanity he's lost? "It's like my eyes are open and I'm looking at you," he tells the girl. "But I'm dead. They pulled out whatever it was inside of me."

Unfortunately, most of the film's subtleties are lost in its second half. As inevitable as it is, the final shootout—with both men in full uniform—is a bit of a letdown. We want to know more about these characters, their struggles, and the ramifications of the violent paths they've chosen. Instead, we get only shotgun blasts and blood-spattered walls. Moodwise, *Rolling Thunder* echoes some of the "disaffected vet" noir films of the post–World War II era, such as George Marshall's *The Blue Dahlia* (1946) and Fred Zinnemann's *Act of Violence* (1948). As shot by cinematographer Jordan Cronenweth (*Cutter's Way* [1981], *Blade Runner* [1982]), the border towns of *Rolling Thunder* are noirish hellholes full of neon lights and deep shadows. The villains, in particular Askew (*Cool Hand Luke*

Tommy Lee Jones portrayed Sgt. John Vohden as a silently seething time bomb, waiting for a reason to explode on the homefront.

MAJOR CHARLES RANE HAS COME HOME TO WAR!

ROLLING THUNDER

ANOTHER SHATTERING EXPERIENCE FROM THE AUTHOR OF "TAXI DRIVER."

Samuel Z. Arkoff presents A LAWRENCE GORDON PRODUCTION
WILLIAM DEVANE starring in "ROLLING THUNDER"
also starring TOMMY LEE JONES · LINDA HAYNES
Executive Producer LAWRENCE GORDON · Produced by NORMAN T. HERMAN · Directed by JOHN FLYNN
Screenplay by PAUL SCHRADER and HEYWOOD GOULD · Story by PAUL SCHRADER
Music by BARRY DeVORZON · Color by DELUXE® Color prints by MOVIELAB
Released by AMERICAN INTERNATIONAL PICTURES

[1967], *Pat Garrett & Billy the Kid* [1973]), are truly frightening. His Automatic Slim is a tough, unrepentant career criminal and Vietnam vet himself, who looks quite up to the task of killing both the heroes. "Now don't give me any of that officer hard shit," he tells Rane. "'Cause I was right there in 'Nam with the rest, 'cept I was lying facedown in the mud while you cats was flying over."

This was Flynn's fourth film as a director, coming on the heels of *The Outfit*, an adaptation of one of Donald E. Westlake's Richard Stark novels. Flynn had begun his career as an assistant to director Robert Wise on *Odds Against Tomorrow* (1959), then later served as John Sturges's assistant on *The Great Escape* (1963). After *Rolling Thunder*, he would go on to make a dozen more theatrical and television movies before his death in 2007.

While the original story and first draft of *Rolling Thunder* were written by Schrader, much of the film's character development was provided by first-time screenwriter Heywood Gould (*Fort Apache the Bronx* [1981]), who was brought in to do a rewrite. The scenes between Rane and his son and the torture reenactment are all Gould's. Schrader has criticized the final film for abandoning his idea of Rane's odyssey as a metaphor for the Vietnam War. Instead of a film about fascism, Schrader said, it became "a fascist film." That's too simplistic a dismissal though. The film can be read either way. In Schrader's version of the shootout, Rane and Vohden gun down criminals and innocents alike, before Rane himself is killed. The ending, as reworked by Flynn and Gould, is no less violent, but more conventional. As filmed, the gun battle is chaotic but expertly choreographed, and only the bad guys go down. Our heroes stumble out of the brothel bloody and bullet-ridden, but alive. "Let's go home," Rane says. (In the novelization of the film, written by Gould under the pen name Richard L. Graves, the two survive the gunfight but Rane dies of his injuries afterward. The novel also has a prologue set in 1966, on the day he was shot down.)

The film was originally produced and skedded for release by 20th Century-Fox, who balked at the extreme violence of the final cut. Following a disastrous test screening in San Jose, the film's producer, Lawrence Gordon, sold it to Samuel Z. Arkoff at American International Pictures. (The novelization, published by Pocket Books in March 1977, still credits it as a 20th Century-Fox production.) The film was released in the fall of that year under an R rating with only minimal cuts. It became a surprise hit, reportedly earning $130 million back on a budget of $5 million. *Rolling Thunder* made Gene Siskel's Ten Best of 1977 list, alongside *Annie Hall*, *Saturday Night Fever*, and *Star Wars*. Quentin Tarantino took the film's title as the name for his short-lived company that rereleased cult movies (such as *Switchblade Sisters* [1975] and *Detroit 9000* [1973]), though the film itself never made the cut. It's now available as a Blu-ray from Shout! Factory, with a featurette that includes interviews with Devane, Jones, Schrader, and Gould. Forty-six years since its release, *Rolling Thunder* holds up as both a time capsule of 1970s cinema and a snapshot of post-Vietnam American madness. ∎

PRIME CUTS: MY FAVORITE NEO-NOIR
Andy Wolverton

Richard Fleischer may not be the first name that comes to mind when listing film noir's greatest directors, but his noir credentials are impressive. After directing two successful B-pictures at RKO, the amnesia noir *The Clay Pigeon* (1949) and *Bodyguard* (1948), Fleischer moved to Eagle-Lion for *Trapped* (1949) before returning to RKO for *Follow Me Quietly* (1949). The director cited this film as a turning point, stating, "This is the film that, above all, increased my knowledge of the trade. I learned how to organize a film."

Fleischer took advantage of the knowledge and skills he learned during *Follow Me Quietly* to direct other notable noir titles *Armored Car Robbery* (1950), *His Kind of Woman* (1951, uncredited), *The Narrow Margin* (1952), and *Violent Saturday* (1955), as well as true crime pictures with strong noir elements: *Compulsion* (1959), a fictionalized account of the 1924 Leopold and Loeb murder trial, and *The Boston Strangler* (1968), loosely based on the story of serial killer Albert DeSalvo. Yet the director once told Eddie Muller that *10 Rillington Place* (1971), the story of British serial killer John Christie, was the "most noir film" he'd ever made.

10 Rillington Place not only retains the actual names of the principal players, but also used dialogue taken from documented sources and was filmed in the London location where the murders took place. Yet the film's relevance far surpasses most stories "based on actual events." Adapted from the book *Ten Rillington Place* (1961) by Ludovic Kennedy, Clive Exton's screenplay walks a fine line be-

British serial killer John Christie is portrayed by Richard Attenborough in one of his finest, most disturbing performances.

tween true crime and horror, adding an examination of two topics of ongoing debate: abortion and capital punishment.

John Christie (Richard Attenborough) is simultaneously the film's most fascinating and disturbing character. In the story's opening, set in 1944, Christie lures a local acquaintance named Muriel (Phyllis MacMahon) into his Notting Hill flat, assuring the woman that he can cure her bronchitis with a method apparently dismissed by most doctors. Donning owllike glasses and speaking mostly in calm whispers with a slight lisp, Christie presents himself as an intelligent yet reserved middle-aged man seeking only to help Muriel. Had this scene taken place in an actual medical facility, we might trust Christie completely. The unshakable confidence he displays with his patient invites a certain level of assurance. Yet the audience suspects what Muriel does not, that the gas delivered by a rubber tube is meant to debilitate rather than relax the young woman. Too late, Muriel comes to the realization that Christie's intent is not to help her but to end her life for his own twisted sexual gratification.

Jumping to 1949, Christie and his wife, Ethel (Pat Heywood), rent out their property's upper-story flat to a young family: Timothy (John Hurt) and Beryl Evans (Judy Geeson) and their infant daughter. Timothy seems reluctant to accept this squalid dwelling in such an uninviting neighborhood, yet Christie's quietly manipulative method of influencing the Evanses, informing them there's another couple "very keen" on the place, rush them into accepting. Learning that Timothy can neither read nor write ignites opportunities for further machinations in Christie's mind. Although five years have passed in the narrative, the film's opening scene remains fresh in the viewer's mind, spurring fears about what crimes Christie may unleash on the unsuspecting Evans family.

Christie and Evans are both liars, but miles apart in their degrees of deception. At a local pub, Timothy boasts of his job and sexual prowess, yet the regulars can see right through him, knowing that his stories are nothing more than wishful fantasies. Timothy is forced to step up his lying game after Christie promises Beryl that he can perform her abortion (illegal at the time in the UK), but instead kills and sexually assaults

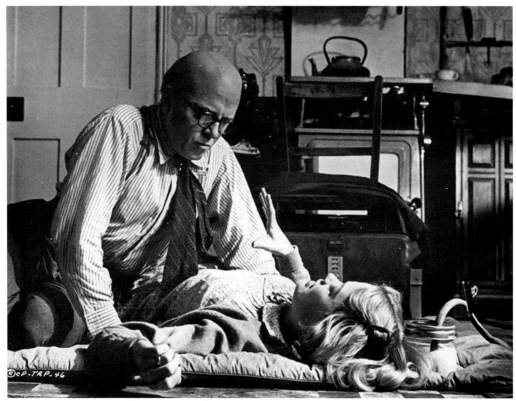
Beryl Evans (Judy Geeson) realizes too late that Christie is about to make her his next victim.

her. Yet Christie is a master liar and manipulator, explaining to Timothy that Beryl's abortion was not only unsuccessful but also the cause of her death. Christie's fabricated lament—"If she had only come to me sooner"—both excuses himself and places the blame on Evans. Christie uses Timothy's anger and confusion to further spin the situation in a way that makes the husband complicit. "So who are the police going to believe?" Christie taunts, "You? Or me, that was a special constable for four years?" The killer then instructs Timothy to stay with his aunt and uncle near Cardiff, telling him to make up some story to appease them. Now, with much more at stake than deceiving a few mates at the pub, Timothy realizes how difficult it is to lie when you're not very good at it.

Christie also understands that Timothy's impulsive nature will help falsely implicate him. Earlier scenes of the couple arguing give evidence of Timothy's rage and lack of control as he shouts and breaks objects in the flat. These episodes are also loud enough to be overheard by neighbors, supporting Christie's later testimony that Timothy is a violent man who could easily have strangled Beryl in a fit of anger. Christie may portray himself as a calm, middle-aged gentleman, but he is instead a cold, calculating manipulator who will do anything to help shift the blame from himself to Timothy.

With fabricated evidence and twisted statements coming primarily from Christie, Timothy's murder trial proves to be a juggernaut that totally overwhelms the helpless young man. While Christie's victims had little time to react to the truth of what was happening to them, Evans is given the opportunity to defend himself but lacks the capacity to do so.

In no time at all, Evans is convicted and sentenced to be executed for the murder of his wife and young daughter (whom Christie also killed). As much as the audience is filled with escalating turmoil at this injustice, the greatest injustice of all occurs as Evans is swiftly taken to a small room, hooded, noosed, and hanged in a matter of seconds. Perhaps even more chilling is the fact that the film's technical advisor, Albert Pierrepoint, was actually the man who executed Evans. Years later, after Christie was convicted of killing

Timothy Evans (John Hurt) has little time to think in the final moments before his execution.

Beryl, Evans's wrongful execution was one of the primary reasons why capital punishment was abolished in the UK in 1965, and it still stands as a sobering moment for contemporary audiences.

Fleischer's previous true crime pictures were all based on twentieth-century cases in the United States, but *10 Rillington Place* forgoes not only American settings, but also more lurid subjects from Britain's own history as represented in such earlier works as David Lean's *Madeleine* (1950), John Gilling's *The Flesh and the Fiends* (1960), and a whole host of Jack the Ripper movies, all of which are set in the nineteenth century. This film draws much of its disturbing atmosphere from a backdrop of fear and desperation resulting from World War II. The fact that the site of the murders was still standing as Fleischer was filming gives harsh evidence that this atrocity was true, and its presence provided a warning that its horror was still evident. (The site of the murders was demolished soon after the film was completed, removing any physical reminders of the tragedies that took place there.)

The almost complete absence of a musical score heightens the horror and tragedy of the murders, not only as the victims' confidence and trust in Christie are ripped away, but also as the intimacy of their final experiences continues to haunt us: Christie's craggy breathing resonating in our ears, his alarming black eyes inches from our own, and the dismal surroundings closing in on us.

10 Rillington Place contains no hint of the sensationalism frequently found in true crime films. Its faithfulness to the events, the documented words spoken, and the location makes the film far more chilling than most of the stories we see based on actual incidents. When the film is over, we feel that we have stood in the same flat where Muriel and Beryl were violated and murdered. We hear Christie's whispers, and we—like Timothy Evans—stand watching the preparations for an execution that we are powerless to prevent. In all these ways and more, Fleischer puts the "true" back in true crime through an unwavering commitment to authenticity, delivering one of cinema's most disturbing and horrific films based on actual events. ∎

PRIME CUTS: MY FAVORITE NEO-NOIR
Adam Nayman

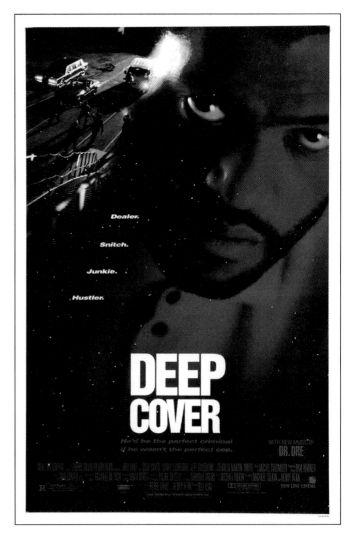

The credit sequence of Bill Duke's *Deep Cover* (1992) unfolds over a static, slow-motion shot of two men smoking crack, quietly ecstatic, sunlight bleeding through shuttered windows. The contrast between the jerky movements of the characters and the skittering funk drums on the soundtrack creates a surreal effect. Time and reality seem out of joint. Speaking with the *Los Angeles Times* at the time of the film's release, Duke—an actor and transplanted TV director whose film debut, *A Rage in Harlem* (1991), had played at Cannes—clarified the meaning and feeling behind the sequence that, as his interviewer pointed out, focused on characters outside the main flow of the narrative—a fact that only made it seem weirder in retrospect.

"Well, they were the leads of the film to me in the sense that these are the people that are being impacted by what I'm going to show you," said Duke. "I was into drugs at one time and drugs are no joke. And withdrawing from drugs is a full-time, 100% courageous act. If you were into alcohol and drugs, it takes a lot to kick that."

The ravages of addiction and the moral turpitude of the War on Drugs

Bill Duke (right) directs Laurence Fishburne and Victoria Dillard during the film's climactic courtroom sequence.

in the glossed-over Reagan Eighties provide a conjoined dramatic and sociological backdrop for *Deep Cover*. The film was released at a turning point for mainstream African American cinema and bore a significant share of period signifiers in the form of its hip-hop soundtrack, which featured songs produced and performed by N. W. A mastermind Dr. Dre and the debut of future genre superstar Snoop Doggy Dogg. *Deep Cover* was distributed by New Line Cinema, the era's exemplary mini-major studio and the one with its ear closest to the ground in terms of Black audiences. Where *A Rage in Harlem*'s crime story had luxuriated in 1950s period detail (and music cues), *Deep Cover*'s hip-hop–saturated storytelling constituted a throwback on a more abstract plane; the film's ardent, multidirectional sense of alienation yoked it even more closely to postwar pulp than its predecessor. Boldly eschewing both gangsta pandering and triumphant blaxploitation pastiche, Duke's film was smart, ruthless, and serious; it didn't attempt to transcend its B-movie trappings so much as trust them to lead the way toward profundity.

There's an enduring sturdiness to the idea of a decent man trapped behind enemy lines—a combat-film conceit that Duke and his screenwriters, Henry Bean and Michael Tolkin, reconfigured for maximum contemporary resonance. *Deep Cover* unfolds a complex—though never convoluted—urban neo-noir scenario in which operatives of the DEA, LAPD, and various West Coast drug cartels become embedded in an intricate, incestuous roundelay of false and real allegiances, all under the sign of vertically integrated capitalism. As in Bean's previous script for *Internal Affairs* (1990), the central police station is a hothouse of influence and intrigue; the next fully honest cop who walks in the door will be the first.

Enter Russell Stevens (Laurence Fishburne), a hard-edged Cincinnati patrolman who's considered by the department to be damaged goods, yet faces his superiors with the kind of ramrod confidence that suggests the system is more broken than the man. Sized up as a solid candidate for undercover work and thrown into the deep end of L.A.'s drug trade without much in the way of preparation, Russell lays his cards on the table for us—and himself—in a voice-over where he vows not to die a junkie like his father, a tragedy presented in an elegiac, snow-flecked flashback.

Jeff Goldblum (right) turns the tables on an unsuspecting Fishburne. The relationship between their characters was expanded from the source novel.

Specifically, Russell has been enlisted to penetrate the multitiered operation of a South America–based importer with government ties (a detail that connects the script loosely to a 1990 nonfiction book of the same name). Now renamed John Hull and effectively deputized to sling coke at his discretion, Russell gets lucky right off the bat by haplessly acquiring a load of false product and beating the charges as a result, and eventually endearing himself to a network of dope brokers who respect his tight-lipped attitude. As he moves up in the underworld, Russell's burgeoning status bumps up against his own Just-Say-No rhetoric, as well as his deepening suspicion that his handlers, observing his progress at safe remove, have even less interest in playing fair than the bad guys.

In 1992, Fishburne was thirty-one years old but already a staple of Black cinema, having starred for Spike Lee in *School Daze* (1988) and John Singleton in *Boyz n the Hood* (1991); he'd also acted for Abel Ferrara in the violent and racially charged gangster drama *King of New York* (1990, distributed by New Line Cinema) whose cinematographer, the Montenegro-born Bojan Bazelli, was hired by Duke to duplicate the film's color-coded expressionism. Shot on location in Los Angeles in the wake of the Rodney King beating, *Deep Cover*'s imagery splits the difference between street-level realism and a grim enchantment; its nightscapes come edged in florid, fluorescent primary colors, as vivid as *Dick Tracy* (1990) but considerably less cartoony. It's a beautiful-looking movie, and Russell—by turns swaggering and furtive, always alert to his environment and the people moving in and out of it—makes for a captivating and savvy tour guide. What makes Fishburne's performance so engaging is how attuned he is toward the *idea* of performance; the disparity between Russell's outward actions as John Hull and his inner monologue takes the strange, disjunctive aesthetic of the opening credits and projects it forward as a tortured character study. By skillfully hiding and finessing his identity depending on the company he keeps—not only with his criminal associates but also his upwardly mobile art-dealer lover (Victoria Dillard), who has little compunction about laundering blood money—is Russell protecting his true self, or losing it? Can he tell the difference? Can we?

As good as Fishburne is in a role that keeps him on-screen for nearly every scene—and requires him to vibrate with barely suppressed paranoia at all times—he graciously cedes certain sequences to his costars. *Deep Cover*'s ace in the hole is Jeff Goldblum, whose mobbed-up Jewish lawyer David Jason is a spiritual predecessor to Sean Penn's indelible cartel attorney David Kleinfeld in *Carlito's Way* (1993). In narrative terms, Russell is the interloper in David's (under)world, but in a movie made by a Black filmmaker and featuring predominantly Black characters, David carries a considerable—and contradictory—burden: he's simultaneously a figure of envy, enmity, and solidarity, and Goldblum, at the time as much an axiom of white and nerdy as Fishburne was of streetwise stoicism, contributes an electrifying performance. Grinning, twitching, and offhandedly misquoting Delmore Schwartz— "with dreams begin responsibilities"—David is as irrepressible as Russell is tightly wound, and he exults in his open contradictions, the desire he expresses to his wife to have his cake and eat it too. One minute, he's copping to his own unapologetic racial fetishism ("How come I like balling Black chicks so much?" he asks, non-rhetorically); the next, he's essaying a progressive (if not quite egalitarian) vision of an America where ethnicity has been fully supplanted, once and for all, by a color-blind profit motive. "The three of us are rich," he explains to a pair of associates during a tense moment. "We're on the same side."

No less than bigger and more commercial hits like *48 Hrs.* (1982) or *Lethal Weapon* (1987), *Deep Cover* is a buddy movie, and it uses the Fishburne-Goldblum pairing to score plenty of laughs amid the carnage. It also wrings real pathos out of Russell's ultimate betrayal of a friend who, for all his faults—and David is nothing if not a repository of flaws, big and small—never sold him out. The climax is powerful not simply because of how smartly it's engineered on a story level—with multiple plotlines intersecting and imploding with tragic consequences—but how it allows Russell to shed various layers of allegiance and obligation without letting him off the hook. Forgotten, abandoned, and severed—by his own hand—from an earnest (if scarily pressurized) friendship, he's forced to confront what, or who, is left over, and who is responsible for "the spoils of fucking war." It's a testament to the film's honestly wrought ambivalence that the coda feels punctuated with a question mark. In the end, there's no sense of resolution, and certainly not of victory—not within the system, and not over it, either. The battle that Duke is depicting features only casualties and survivors; what makes *Deep Cover* powerful is how it understands how narrow—and jagged— the margins can be. ■

PRIME CUTS: MY FAVORITE NEO-NOIR
Thomas Burchfield

STRAW DOGS

S am Peckinpah's *Straw Dogs*. Saying those four words among any group of thoughtful cineastes guarantees a response: faces turn pale, mouths grimace, eyes shift sideways. Even the director's fervent admirers often cringe, shuffle their feet, and look away. "Oh. *That*." And then they turn to safer topics—*The Killer Elite* (1975), *Bring Me the Head of Alfredo Garcia* (1974), and even *Convoy* (1978).

There are good reasons. *Straw Dogs* is like a cobra coiled in the middle of your living room—no looking away, no getting rid of it. All you can do is step around and move on.

The labels pasted on the film since its Christmas 1971 release raid the dark pages of the thesaurus: "repellent," "misogynistic," "misanthropic," "fascist," "nihilistic," "reactionary," "depressing," "mean-spirited," "badly contrived," "cruel," "ham-fisted," "wrong-headed," "ultra-cynical," and of course, "problematic." "Controversial" also heads the list—then, now, and forever. Some of those labels fit. But you can also call *Straw Dogs* "powerful," "brilliant," "angry," "intelligent," "insightful," "incisive," "nuanced," "anguished," "serious," and finally: a gem of vicious poetry, admirable yet wholly unlovable. Few serious films have ignited such extremes of praise and damnation. Regarding genre categories, it's been called a

Western (due to Peckinpah's reputation), a psychological thriller, a domestic drama of a troubled marriage, a home invasion movie, and an existential howl.

You can also call it noir. Every serious noirista owes this film at least one look.

Straw Dogs is a "rural noir." Its setting is Wakely, an English village in Cornwall—a smudge on the map, like those Texas towns in Jim Thompson novels such as *Pop. 1280* (1964) or *The Killer Inside Me* (1952)—poor, dismal, sunk in corruption. The only law is a one-armed constable (T. P. McKenna). The real power lies with a gang of lowlifes, headed by Tom Hedden (Peter Vaughan).

The film is steeped in dread from its opening shot, a blurry image that, when sharpened into focus, reveals children romping in a cemetery while the credits fade in and out, underlined by composer Jerry Fielding's ominous fanfare. The camera turns from this portentous symbol to the dame, a voluptuous sex kitten named Amy Sumner (Susan George, in a courageous performance), striding bralessly along and confident in her sensuality, a beauty queen come home again. Not much older than the kids in the cemetery, she's as lusciously feline as Ava Gardner in *The Killers* (1946). And yet, unlike other femme fatales, her mature exterior covers a troubling innocence.

Next comes the chump: the husband Amy's brought home with her, David Sumner (Dustin Hoffman). A character out of *Detour* (1945) or *D.O.A.* (1950), David stands apart from those dupes as a privileged sort: an American academic fleeing Vietnam-era violence, in search of some peace and quiet where he can finish his thesis on stellar structures. Or maybe he just wants to keep his head in the stars forever. Like Amy, David is a child, but unlike her, he has no place to call home. He's a vulnerable stranger here, clutching a box of groceries like a shield. He knows he's married far out of his league, to a woman with whom he has nothing in common. Now he's compounded his error by following her into this forbidding world.

Amy and David live a few miles outside the village, in her late father's home, Trencher's Farm,

Dustin Hoffman in a reflective moment on the set with director Sam Peckinpah.

Susan George, one of the most prolific actors of the early 1970s, had the most challenging role of her career as the conflicted provocative Amy Sumner.

where, as she reminds him, "Every chair is my daddy's chair." The whole world around is, in fact, hers. As it tugs her back into its embrace, David's alienation deepens. He treats his wife and her people with passive-aggressive snobbery, further fueling the villagers' contempt for the outsider who married their beauty queen.

Meanwhile, Amy has hired her ex-lover Charlie Venner (Del Henney) and his loutish mates (colorful gutter trash in classic Peckinpah style) to fix their garage roof. Rather than work, they ogle Amy while creeping around inside the house with impunity. Eventually, they kill Amy's cat and hang the corpse in a closet. But David and Amy are too paralyzed to confront these lowlifes.

As Amy grows infuriated by David's withdrawal and passivity, she finds herself drawn back to Venner. Right behind Venner, though, loom his mates—one of whom, Scutt (Ken Hutchison), also has his eye on Amy. In a flailing attempt at peacemaking, David accepts the gang's invitation to a hunting trip in the moorlands. There, they abandon him and sneak back to Trencher's Farm, where Venner and Scutt rape Amy, a scene that remains among the most shocking acts of cinematic violence—as Peckinpah and his collaborators fully intended.

The Sumner marriage ends. With her faith in David gone, Amy can't even tell him what has happened. David fires Venner and company, but it's too late. Later, the couple attend an evening village fete (one masterfully edited sequence among many), where Amy finds herself surrounded by her attackers as memories of her rape dissolve in and out at the edges of the frame. For once, David shows some feeling and takes her home early. But while driving through the night fog (one of several contrivances), they happen to run over Henry Niles (David Warner), the village idiot who's fleeing after accidentally killing Janice (Sally Thomsett), Tom Hedden's slatternly young daughter.

The Sumners innocently take him home and call down to the village for help. The Hedden gang gets word and loads themselves up with booze and shotguns to lay siege to the Sumner house, bringing us into the world of *The Desperate Hours* (1955) and *The Night of the Hunter* (1955). David, confronted with the truth of his life, must now fight for that life, armed only with his own cunning, his enemies' drunken underestimation of him, and a conveniently placed mantrap.

Credible or not, the siege is extraordinary filmmaking, shot and edited in unnerving rhythms of noirish light and shadow. So many action sequences since then—many using Peckinpah's techniques—leave viewers confused, irritated, and even bored. But *Straw Dogs* gets every shot and every cut right, timed to the split second. You know exactly—and horribly—where you are. Pitifully few action directors are the equal of Sam Peckinpah, then or now.

The end of the film lacks any sense of macho triumph. David's brief flush of pride after the seige fades as he takes in the catastrophe he helped bring on with his own passivity. Only moments before, he proudly stood his ground declaring, "I will not allow violence against this house!" while we stare down at him as though he were a pompous little boy. But this was never his house. He's killed these men simply because they bullied and humiliated him too hard, too often.

Many noir films compromise their bleakness with hopeful endnotes. Not *Straw Dogs*. It strikes a perfect final note of noir darkness as David leaves Amy alone among the dead to drive Niles through the night to safety.

"I don't know my way home," Niles says.

"That's alright," David replies with an enigmatic smile. "I don't either."

David is lost once again, only now he knows it. As he and Niles vanish in the night, it's clear that, like many a noir protagonist, he's lost for good.

With a genuine auteur like Peckinpah at the helm there's much to praise, including the director's skill with his actors (particularly Hoffman and George), John Coquillon's blue-tinged cinematography and lighting, and Fielding's astounding score. The superb editing team included Robert Wolfe, a Peckinpah staple, and future director Roger Spottiswoode. But despite its aesthetic virtues, *Straw Dogs* is not quite a great film. Based on a bad suspense novel, the script by David Z. Goodman and Peckinpah plays like a thesis out to score ideological points, similar to John Wayne–Jane Fonda agit-prop movies of the same era.

But those films at least offer some hope, with Fonda pointing left and Wayne pointing right. *Straw Dogs* offers none, only violent oblivion. It strives bravely and awkwardly to go beyond current politics and for its unique dramatic circumstance to serve as a metaphor for life. The power of its filmmaking badgers the viewer into a nihilistic corner. You think you're a tough guy? *Straw Dogs* might leave you quivering in despair.

The cruelty shows most in the characterizations of David and Amy. You feel sorry for *D.O.A*'s Frank Bigelow and *Detour*'s Al Roberts, even identify with them in a there-but-for-the-grace-of-God-go-I manner. (Fredric March and his family in *The Desperate Hours* are a Middle-American bastion against noir chaos as personified by Humphrey Bogart.) Yet despite George's excellence Amy garners little sympathy. David receives absolutely none. Peckinpah admitted that he saw them as the villains, but the Sumners deserve some compassion for their youthful naivete. The film is having none of it. Innocence, even among the young, is a crime.

We're all killers, Peckinpah declares with his unmistakable snarl. Case closed. And so, *Straw Dogs* takes a place of troubled honor in noir's heart of darkness. ∎

PRIME CUTS: MY FAVORITE NEO-NOIR
Steve Kronenberg

TARGETS

Targets (1968) is as important as it is underrated. It was writer-director Peter Bogdanovich's first feature film, and while it's generally viewed as an anti-gun polemic, its tone, theme, and style mark it as a genuine neo-noir. Taking a cue from *Sunset Boulevard* (1950), Bogdanovich infused his screenplay with a "meta" mindset, casting Boris Karloff as an elderly horror film veteran on the verge of retirement. *Targets* also takes noir into uncharted territory, cleverly conflating the end of Hollywood's Golden Age with the cynicism and dissolution that would begin to plague the United States in the late 1960s.

Playing a mirror image of himself, Karloff is Byron Orlok, an aging bogeyman who feels irrelevant and outdated. Bogdanovich cast himself as Sammy Michaels, the director of Orlok's last film, *The Terror* (which is in fact a slapdash 1963 production Karloff made for B-movie icon Roger Corman). While meeting with Michaels to discuss his impending retirement, Orlok scans a newspaper headline about a mass murder and realizes that the harmless cinematic horrors of the 1930s pale in comparison to the atrocities occurring in contemporary America. "My kind of horror isn't horror anymore," he laments. At Michaels's urging, Orlok reluctantly agrees to a final personal appearance at a screening of *The Terror*, to be held at Los Angeles's Reseda Drive-In. He's also in the crosshairs of a rifle held by a young man named Bobby Thompson (Tim O'Kelly), who's testing his aim while purchasing the piece from a gun shop located across the street from Michaels's office. "I always wanted a rifle like this," he tells the shopkeeper, before adding it to an arsenal stored in the trunk of his car. Thompson's boyish persona and squeaky-clean garb mask a disturbed soul. Living a dull, placid life in an L.A. suburb, he seethes with frustration. "I don't know what's happening to me," he tells his wife (Tanya Morgan). "I get funny ideas." Suddenly and without provocation or motive, he robotically guns down his wife, his mother, and a teen delivering groceries before embarking on a shooting spree that takes him from the San Diego Freeway to the Reseda Drive-In and a climactic confrontation with Orlok.

Though shot in late 1967, *Targets* wasn't released until August 1968, mere months after the assassinations of Martin Luther King Jr. and Robert Kennedy. The film bears a sensibility both wistful and frightening, augmented by fine performances from Karloff and O'Kelly. Disabled and frail, the eighty-year-old Karloff effectively captures Orlok's disillusion, coupling avuncular amiability with bitterness and heartbreak. His interplay with Bogdanovich and Nancy Hsueh, who plays his assistant, is especially poignant. Karloff's sad eyes were always those of a monster with a soul. (His beautifully rendered one-take recitation of the Arabian fable "Appointment in Samarra" drew a standing ovation from the film's cast and crew.) Bogdanovich's script touched Karloff deeply, and he agreed to offer additional days of service for free. He lived just long enough to enjoy lavish praise for his performance before his death on February 2, 1969, at age eighty-one.

Karloff embodies the film's elegiac tone, but it's O'Kelly's laconic loner who gives *Targets* its unnerving edge. Thompson is an amalgam of the mediocre and the monstrous. His performance is free of pretense and artifice, stripped down to underplayed, faceless psychopathy. We cringe as we see him sipping a soda while coolly picking off motorists on the San Diego Freeway and families at the Reseda Drive-In. Thompson's well-scrubbed looks and obsession with guns may remind noir fans of

Boris Karloff and Peter Bogdanovich discuss horrors past and present in this candid shot taken during filming.

Bart Tare in *Gun Crazy* (1950), but Thompson lacks Tare's vulnerability. He's more a taciturn Norman Bates.

Targets owes much of its noir acidity to Bogdanovich's somber style and László Kovács's gritty cinematography. Kovács's camera trails Thompson through Los Angeles's grimiest neighborhoods, grimly depicting a flat, soulless landscape that mirrors the gunman's own emotional void. When Thompson murders his family, Kovács comes in tight and close, using POV shots to emphasize the scene's random brutality. He weaponizes the zoom lens, using it to capture each of Thompson's victims through the crosshairs of a rifle just before the trigger is pulled. Bogdanovich's then-wife, Polly Platt, who also co-wrote the picture, assisted Kovács in devising appropriate lighting for both lead characters: Orlok is surrounded by warm, white hues, while Thompson's nondescript killer is bathed in bland blues and impenetrable darkness, a ghostly silhouette skulking through his suburban home. (Platt cited the simplicity of Don Siegel's noirs as a primary stylistic influence.) Kovács's visual imagination turns the film's final scene into a hallucinatory nightmare. We see Thompson's drive-in massacre through his eyes, as we watch the real Orlok advancing toward him while the celluloid Orlok stalks the sets of *The Terror* on the theater's enormous screen.

Unlike *The Sniper* (1952), another noir about a serial shooter, *Targets* is not focused on police procedure or psychological profiling. We know little about Bobby Thompson and even less about his pathology. Bogdanovich's approach is cold and detached, suffused with an unsettling quietude. The only concession to a soundtrack is the occasional source music emanating from the radio in Thompson's car. Family gatherings at his home are deceptively reserved and restrained. Credit Bogdanovich, Kovács, and sound editor Verna Fields for the film's crucial freeway scene. As Thompson opens fire on his unsuspecting victims, we hear only ambient noise: wind, traffic, gunshots. The effect is realistic, disturbing, and eerily prescient.

Thompson confronts his doomed wife in this eerie scene from *Targets*.

Ever the movie lover, Bogdanovich top-loads *Targets* with subtle homages to Golden Age cinema, connecting the demise of old-school filmmaking with America's gradual loss of innocence. Byron Orlok is named after the vampire count in F. W. Murnau's horror classic *Nosferatu* (1922). Karloff is seen perusing and praising his own performance in Howard Hawks's *The Criminal Code* (1931). Thompson's doomed family watches a television ad for a showing of Otto Preminger's *Anatomy of a Murder* (1959). In a nod to the finale of *White Heat* (1949), Thompson conducts his highway massacre while perched atop an oil tank. The entrance to the now-demolished Reseda Drive-In was shot at night, aglow in 1950s neon. Children cavort on its playground while families munch popcorn and await the start of the show. A projectionist opens film cans and loads 35mm reels onto the drive-in's massive projector. Juxtaposed with the carnage on-screen, these images symbolize the end of an era.

In the TCM podcast "The Plot Thickens," Bogdanovich told Ben Mankiewicz that *Targets* evolved from an idea hatched by Roger Corman. After completing *The Terror*, Karloff still owed Corman two

Terror Times Two: Real-life monster Thompson is juxtaposed with cinematic frightmeister Byron Orlok (Karloff).

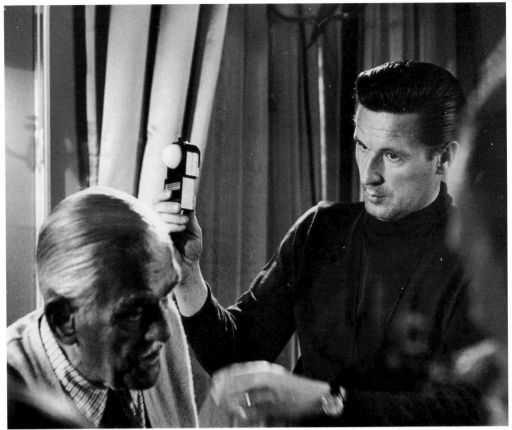
A beaming Karloff pauses as ace DP László Kovács adjusts the lighting between scenes.

more days of work. At the time, Bogdanovich was employed as Corman's assistant, directing second unit material and rewriting the script for the director's biker opus *The Wild Angels* (1966). Corman offered the fledgling filmmaker $6,000 to write and direct an 80-minute feature, incorporating twenty minutes of fresh Karloff footage, twenty minutes of unused Karloff footage from *The Terror*, and forty minutes of footage with a newly chosen supporting cast.

Bogdanovich and Platt's original treatment envisioned Karloff as a masked serial killer. Harold Hayes, who'd been editing Bogdanovich's essays on film for *Esquire*, wisely advised him to scrap the script and base his story on Charles Whitman's shocking mass shooting at the University of Texas. Whitman was a boyish, twenty-five-year-old former UT Austin student and Marine Corps sharpshooter. Years of childhood abuse by his father took a terrible psychological toll. On August 1, 1966, after murdering his wife and mother, Whitman armed himself with a cache of guns and ascended the campus observation tower, killing three university employees along the way. When he reached the top, he began randomly shooting at people on the ground. Within a span of 96 minutes, he killed fourteen people and injured thirty-one more before two Austin police officers were able to confront him and shoot him dead. The atrocity stunned Americans and prompted demands for gun control and police departments on college campuses.

Bogdanovich took Hayes's advice and rewrote his screenplay, using Whitman as a model for Bobby Thompson. Like Whitman, Thompson prepares a suicide note before beginning his rampage, methodically places his family's corpses in a bedroom, and talks about "killing some pigs." Karloff would no longer serve as the film's killer; instead, he'd portray a world-weary frightmeister ready to retire. "I laughed and I thought 'wait a second,'" Bogdanovich recalled. "If he's an actor, he doesn't want to make those kinds of movies anymore. There's the beginning of a picture." Bogdanovich also consulted his friend and idol, maverick filmmaker Samuel Fuller, who helped him shape the screenplay and suggested that the film conclude at the Reseda Drive-In with a standoff between Orlok and Thompson. (Fuller generously waived both a fee and screen credit, but Bogdanovich paid him tribute by naming Sammy Michaels after Fuller's first and middle names.) Corman served as executive producer and gave Bogdanovich a $130,000 budget and a twenty-three-day shooting schedule.

Targets was filmed without permits, forcing Bogdanovich and Kovács to "steal" shots throughout Los Angeles and Hollywood. The San Diego Freeway shoot ended in chaos, lending the movie some unexpected authenticity. "You're not allowed to shoot on the freeway," Bogdanovich told Mankiewicz. "We just did it." Kovács used a wide-angle lens and communicated with the director via walkie-talkies. Just before each gunshot was fired, Bogdanovich would yell "bang" into his device. "We actually brought a girl onto the freeway," he recalled. "She got out of the car in the story. And we went 'bang' and she fell, got shot in the back and fell. And that's when the cops came." As the scene ends, viewers can see the unrehearsed appearance of the police on-screen. "[It] was a lot of fun," Bogdanovich remembered, "if you think of blind terror as being fun. Of all my pictures, it was the most consuming."

American International Pictures offered to release *Targets*, but Bogdanovich wanted distribution from a major studio. He showed the film to Paramount chief Robert Evans, who immediately purchased it with the approval of Gulf + Western CEO Charles Bluhdorn. Audience reception was disappointing, but stellar reviews earned the young director's debut effort a cult following. Praising *Targets* as a thriller with a social conscience, Quentin Tarantino has called it "one of the greatest directorial debuts of all time." Criterion has now released the film on Blu-ray, pristinely restored and supplemented with an analysis from Richard Linklater and informative commentaries from Bogdanovich and Platt (though Bogdanovich erroneously states that Charles Whitman committed suicide before the police could get to him).

Targets remains an essential entry in the true crime noir canon, arguably the first film based on an actual mass shooting. As a prediction of chaos to come, it remains more resonant and relevant than ever. Its many allusions to movies and filmmaking anticipate the meta-rich themes of *Day for Night* (1973), *Being John Malkovich* (1999), and *Once Upon a Time in Hollywood* (2019). Its unsparing depictions of gun violence presage *Dirty Harry* (1971) and *Taxi Driver* (1976). As film noir, its icy, documentarian approach to murder and madness recalls such films as *He Walked by Night* (1948), *Follow Me Quietly* (1949), and *Psycho* (1960). Finally, *Targets* is an exercise in irony, celebrating Hollywood's glorious past while prophesying a grim and terrifying future. ∎

BOOK vs. FILM

Ben Terrall

One summer in the late 1940s, future screenwriter Ernest Lehman worked up two short stories from his experiences as a legman for Broadway press agent Irving Hoffman. He sold "Hunseker Fights the World" to *Collier's*; *Cosmopolitan* bought "It's the Little Things That Count."

After this success, Lehman continued to explore the hyperactive milieu of his former job. The result was a novelette he called "The Sweet Smell of Success," featuring Harvey Hunseker, a powerful columnist, and Sidney Wallace, a sycophantic press agent who feeds Hunseker material. That piece of long-form fiction (published in *Cosmopolitan* as "Tell Me About It Tomorrow!"), along with elements from the two earlier stories, would be the source material for one of the best Hollywood movies of the 1950s, *Sweet Smell of Success* (1957).

For years, Lehman's former boss Hoffman, who became a drama critic and columnist for the *Hollywood Reporter* in 1938, fed material to the powerful New York columnist Walter Winchell. Winchell's reach was such that when Lehman's agent attempted to sell his client's story in Hollywood before it appeared in *Cosmopolitan*, no studio heads would touch it. Hoffman wouldn't speak to Lehman for more than a year after the story appeared, but his feelings eventually thawed enough that he let Lehman write an entire column under Hoffman's byline. Lehman used that opportunity to urge Hollywood to make a movie about the sizzling world of Broadway showbiz hustlers, noting that Ernest Lehman was just the guy to write such a picture.

By 1957, Winchell's popularity was on the wane. The possibility of adapting "Tell Me About It Tomorrow!" to film became more likely, especially when Hecht-Hill-Lancaster (HHL)—a production team Burt Lancaster put together with agent Harold Hecht and former MGM writer James Hill—expressed interest. Based on HHL's success with their Oscar-winner *Marty* (1955), Lehman agreed to sell them his story and write the screenplay if he could also direct.

After scouting locations, Lehman was told that United Artists, which would be handling distribution, had cold feet over hiring a first-time director. Lancaster and his partners selected Alexander Mackendrick—whom they had been working with on another project—to replace Lehman at the helm. Given that his filmography largely consisted of British comedies such as *The Man in the White Suit* (1951) and *The Ladykillers* (1955), Mackendrick wasn't the likeliest choice to direct a hardboiled look at the seamy side of New York's theater district. But the versatile Scotsman was a quick study who had spent time in the world of British tabloid journalism and, as he later explained, "had always hankered to make a melodrama, a film noir as it has been called . . . I liked the idea of trying to capture on screen the atmosphere of Manhattan."

Mackendrick felt the script had too many scenes consisting of two seated characters talking, with little sense of the city's frenetic street life. He set about working with Lehman to tell the story in more visual terms. Though most of the characters from the original story remained, Lehman got rid of Sidney's hectoring mother and disapproving brother, making his uncle Frank (Sam Levene) the sole

Tony Curtis tries to impress Burt Lancaster's newspaper columnist. Curtis has the most screen time in the film despite receiving second billing.

Left to right: The imposing Lancaster holds court over Curtis, Martin Milner, and Sam Levene.

voice of familial conscience. The story's Harvey Hunseker became J. J. Hunsecker, and Sidney Wallace became Sidney Falco.

Under the pile-driving pressure of Hecht, Hill, and Lancaster, Lehman developed a spastic colon; the screenwriter's doctor advised him to resign from the production and convalesce somewhere other than Los Angeles. Mackendrick chose Clifford Odets to replace the exhausted Lehman. In the 1930s, Odets was the left-wing golden boy of Broadway, with five plays running in New York simultaneously at the age of twenty-nine. He was now floundering in Hollywood, without a screenplay credit since 1947. Though hired for just a few weeks of dialogue rewrites, his assignment turned into a months-long project.

When shooting on the picture began, Odets was still revising scenes, pounding out dialogue well into the night. Roaming about in the wee hours in the midst of Times Square location work, Tony Curtis, who seemed born to play the role of Sidney Falco, heard noises coming from a prop truck. Inside he found Odets in an overcoat hunched over his typewriter. The revitalized Odets made a lasting impression on Curtis by handing the young actor a page on which he'd just typed the line, "The cat's in the bag, and the bag's in the river." Odets continued to feverishly fine-tune scenes until the final day of principal photography.

Odets's focus on interactions between characters gave Mackendrick leeway to devise cuts and camera moves that enhanced the sizzle of Odets's writing. Odets reassured the director that the cure for any danger of the dialogue seeming too stilted or implausible was to "play the situations, not the words. And play them fast." Odets also advised Curtis that the key to nailing Falco was to be constantly moving, never still.

Mackendrick collaborated closely with ace cinematographer James Wong Howe to achieve the movie's hyperkinetic camera moves. Howe contributed terrific use of the crab dolly and employed

Double-X film, a brand-new stock that made it easier to shoot in low light, giving a high-contrast, classic noir look to the footage shot in Manhattan.

The film's extensive use of New York exteriors made the city itself a prominent character. Buildings were packed tightly behind the players, thanks to the shooting of master shots with long-focus lenses (usually used for close-ups) from far away; close-ups were shot with wide-angle lenses, which kept backgrounds in focus, almost overwhelming the players and amping up the paranoid, noir-as-all-get-out tension. Elmer Bernstein's brassy, swaggering score—written with input from jazz drummer Chico Hamilton (who appears as himself)—nicely enhances the pizzazz and brashness of the film's urban environment.

Lancaster's alpha male behavior on set, including overriding Mackendrick's direction, echoed Hunsecker's will to dominate. The former acrobat's solid, imposing physique contrasted sharply with Lehman's original character, whom Odets describes as "pudgy," with a "fat little mouth." Howe later recalled how his camerawork further enhanced J. J.'s menacing physicality: "Hunsecker was lit so that his chiseled features stood out and his steel-rimmed eyeglasses gave him a sort of owlish look, like a predator."

While in the novelette Hunseker has no interest in politics, *Sweet Smell of Success* shows J. J. giving advice to a US senator and later patriotically praising the "Democratic Way of Life" in rehearsals for his TV show. When his sister Susan's suitor, Steve, bristles under J. J.'s grilling, Hunsecker responds by claiming the young man had disparaged both the columnist and his audience: "That boy wiped his feet on the choice, on the predilections of sixty million men and women of the greatest country in the world!" J. J.'s use of bullying nationalism to manipulate his mass media audience acutely presages the modern day rise of Rupert Murdoch's prevaricating demagogues.

In 1952, Odets had given up the names of six men to the House Un-American Activities Committee. Though all six had already been fingered by Elia Kazan, he didn't feel great about his decision; when Odets gave the eulogy for actor J. Edward Bromberg, one of those he had named, he blamed Bromberg's death on HUAC. It's hard not to conclude that his insertion of an implicit critique of McCarthyism into *Sweet Smell of Success* was an attempt to repent for testifying against his friends.

"Tell Me About It Tomorrow!" closes on a dark note, with Sidney cornered in Hunseker's apartment, the curtain coming down on his fast-talking pursuit of the good life. Mackendrick and HHL battled over the movie's ending, with Mackendrick's version—which won out—showing Falco fleeing the wrath of J. J. only to be hunted down by the brutal cop and Hunsecker flunky Kello (Emile Meyer). The filmmakers threw in a line to placate the Motion Picture Production Code directive that Falco renounce his sinful ways, but Curtis blurting out, "That fat cop can break my bones, but he'll never stop me from telling what I know" doesn't give his terrified character a very convincing halo.

The film's premier drew scores of young fans gaga over Tony Curtis. Curtis gushed that "this is a feel-*bad* movie," but his enthusiasm wasn't shared by the bobby-soxers, who were dismayed by their idol's latest role. Complicated characters making bad choices for personal gain were staples of the classic noir being championed by French critics, but they were still unacceptable to a sizable chunk of ticket buyers.

Critics were mostly put off by the lack of a sympathetic lead character. Posterity has been kinder: while the sunny optimism, heroic male leads, and triumphant virtue of mainstream fifties movies has been mostly relegated to the delusional fantasies of right-wing nostalgists, *Sweet Smell of Success*'s decidedly darker view of our society rings all too true. A major influence on Martin Scorsese, Barry Levinson, and many other writers and directors, the film has stood the test of time and then some. ∎

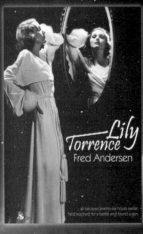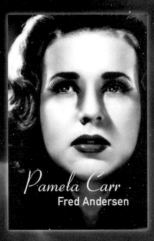

CONTRIBUTORS

Jeremy Arnold is the L.A.-based author of three books in the Turner Classic Movies/Running Press library: *The Essentials Volumes 1 and 2*, and *Christmas in the Movies*. His writing has appeared in other books, *The Hollywood Reporter*, *Variety*, *Moviemaker*, TCM online, and elsewhere. A frequent Blu-ray commentator, he has also appeared on TCM several times as a guest host, including for a 20-film spotlight on B-movies he programmed for the network in 2023.

Thomas Burchfield's short story "Lucky Day" appears in *Berkeley Noir*. Burchfield is the author of *Butchertown*, a 1920s gangland noir novel; *Dragon's Ark*, a contemporary Dracula novel; and four unproduced screenplays published as e-books: *The Uglies*, *Whackers*, *Now Speaks the Devil*, and *Dracula: Endless Night*. He's written for *Filmfax* and *The Strand Magazine*, and is also a film critic for two Medium publications: *Frame Rated* and *Fanfare*. He lives in Northern California with his wife, Elizabeth, and can be found on Facebook.

Danilo Castro is a managing editor of *NOIR CITY* Magazine. He has contributed to several other publications including PopMatters and *Little White Lies*.

Jake Hinkson is the author of several novels, including the recent *Find Him*, as well as the essay collection *The Blind Alley: Exploring Film Noir's Forgotten Corners*. His fiction has been translated into French, German, and Italian. In 2018, his novel *No Tomorrow* was awarded the *Grand Prix des Littératures Policière*, France's most prestigious award for crime and detective fiction.

Vince Keenan is the former Editor-in-Chief of *NOIR CITY* Magazine (2020 - 2022). With his wife Rosemarie Keenan, he writes the Lillian Frost and Edith Head mysteries (*Design for Dying*, *Dangerous to Know*, *The Sharpest Needle*, *Idle Gossip*) under the pen name Renee Patrick. He is also the author of *Down the Hatch: One Man's One Year Odyssey Through Classic Cocktail Recipes and Lore*.

Steve Kronenberg is a managing editor of *NOIR CITY* Magazine. He has served as co-publisher and contributor to the classic horror magazine *Monsters from the Vault* and is co-author of *The Creature Chronicles: Exploring the Black Lagoon Trilogy, Universal Terrors 1951-1955* published by McFarland and Company. Steve is also a contributing writer to the boxing magazine *Ringside Seat* and to the upcoming horror magazine *Cryptology*, whose first issue will release in October 2024.

Adam Nayman is a critic, lecturer, and author based in Toronto. He writes for *The Ringer*, *Reverse Shot*, the *New Yorker*, and *Sight and Sound*, and teaches cinema studies at the University of Toronto. He has written several books on film, including the ECW Pop Classics entry *It Doesn't Suck: Showgirls* and illustrated critical monographs on the Coen brothers, Paul Thomas Anderson, and David Fincher for Abrams.

Imogen Sara Smith, Editor-in-Chief of *NOIR CITY* Magazine since 2023, is the author of *In Lonely Places: Film Noir Beyond the City*. Based in New York City, she writes for *Sight and Sound*, *Film Comment*, *Reverse Shot*, MUBI, The Criterion *Current*, and many other journals, and is a frequent commentator on The Criterion Channel and on Blu-ray discs. Imogen has taught film history at NYU, the School of Visual Arts, and Maine Media Workshops. She is currently working on a biography of Lauren Bacall for Oxford University Press.

Wallace Stroby is an award-winning journalist and the author of 10 novels, the most recent of which is *Heaven's a Lie* (Mulholland Books). Four of his novels feature Crissa Stone, a female professional thief whom Kirkus Reviews calls "Crime fiction's best bad girl ever."

Ben Terrall's writings have appeared in the *NOIR CITY* Magazine, *January Magazine*, the *San Francisco Bay Guardian*, *NACLA Report on the Americas*, the *San Francisco Chronicle*, *In These Times*, *CounterPunch*, and other fine outlets. Terrall thanks his parents and sister Mary for nurturing his movie addiction in his formative toddler years.

Peter Tonguette has written about film, books, and the arts for *The Wall Street Journal*, *The New York Times*, *National Review*, *The Weekly Standard*, *The New Criterion*, *Sight and Sound*, and many other publications. He is a contributing writer at the *Washington Examiner*. The author of books on Orson Welles and James Bridges, he is currently writing a biography of Peter Bogdanovich.

Rachel Walther is a regular contributor to *NOIR CITY* Magazine and the film columnist for *Hamam*, an international arts journal. Her first book, *Born to Lose: The Making of Dog Day Afternoon*, is based on the article in this collection and scheduled for release in Fall 2025 from Headpress UK.

Andy Wolverton is a writer, teacher, and former librarian. He has presented and led discussions of more than 100 films at public libraries, the Annapolis Film Festival, and for online events. His film writing can be found on Substack at *Journeys in Darkness and Light*. Andy is also the author of *Men Don't Read: The Unlikely Story of the Guys Book Club*. He lives in the Annapolis, Maryland area.

John Wranovics is the author of *Chaplin and Agee*. John's writing on film and social history has appeared in *The New York Times*, *Positif*, *Capricci 2011*, *Film Watch*, and various academic anthologies and conferences.

LINGER

HIS STORY IS WRITTEN IN BULLETS BLOOD AND BLONDES!

Featuring

Edmund LOWE • Anne JEFFREYS

Eduardo CIANNELLI • MARC LAWRENCE • ELISHA COOK, Jr.

and Introducing LAWRENCE TIERNEY as John Dillinger

Produced by MAURICE and FRANKLIN KING
Directed by MAX NOSSECK
Screenplay by PHILIP YORDAN